Advance Praise

"What we all need now is some hope. Mel Young is a man who has shown that the most seemingly hopeless situations have solutions. He allows the reader to believe that there is a way to prevail."

Andrea Coleman
Founder and CEO, Two Wheels for Life

"Mel and Alexandra intertwine case studies, personal experience, observation, realism and a healthy dose of optimism to explore how the values of a growing movement of socially and environmentally minded entrepreneurs could form the basis of a better system. It's exciting and energising."

Neil Francis
Entrepreneur and author of *The Entrepreneur's Book*

"We urgently need a new global system: the coronavirus pandemic of 2020 has shed light on the cracks in the current world order. We need a positive way forward and in this practical book, Mel and Alexandra shed a light on a group of disruptors who have been determinedly creating a new, better way forward. Positive change is possible – it's happening already. I should know; I am one of them!"

Chris Underhill MBE
Mentor and serial social entrepreneur

Published by
LID Publishing Limited
The Record Hall, Studio 304,
16-16a Baldwins Gardens,
London EC1N 7RJ, UK

info@lidpublishing.com
www.lidpublishing.com

A member of:

BPR

businesspublishersroundtable.com

Printed by CPI Group (UK) Ltd, Croydon CR0 4YY

ISBN: 978-1-912555-91-8
ISBN: 978-1-911671-16-9 (ebook)

Cover and page design: Caroline Li

Social Entrepreneurship

A better way of thinking about a sustainable future

Mel Young
Alexandra Matthews

LID

MADRID | MEXICO CITY | LONDON
NEW YORK | BUENOS AIRES
BOGOTA | SHANGHAI | NEW DELHI

Contents

Preface

This book is the first in a series.

This book is being published during the global coronavirus pandemic, when much is being written and discussed about how we will return to normal or what a 'new normal' might look like.

We believe that a new normal is imperative for the future of the world. We were writing about this long before the pandemic arrived, but we weren't talking about tinkering around with the current system. Our position is that the current system doesn't work in a modern, global world and that we need to completely reinvent it.

But we don't know what that system looks like. There are some real challenges when you delve into the subject – it is much easier to be critical and negative than it is to be constructive.

Our whole series is based on what this new system might look like and how we can build it.

Where should we start? This first book focuses on social entrepreneurs because they are the people at the coalface around the globe who are coming up with practical solutions. Many of the leading social entrepreneurs are coming together to look at systems change connected with the United Nations Sustainable Development Goals. They are all positive people with a 'can-do' spirit.

So, that's where we start – with positive people who are doing constructive things. We can build so much on top of that.

We have written this book together, drawing on our conversations with social entrepreneurs and the experience of social entrepreneurship. Mel is a leading social entrepreneur himself, and, as such, he wrote Chapters 2, 3 and 4 from his first-hand experience.

There are so many social entrepreneurs having remarkable impact on the world; it is impossible to capture them all in one publication. What we have tried to do is to capture the essence of social entrepreneurialism and why we believe it holds many of the answers to a brighter future. We are both British and based in the UK. Our familiarity with social entrepreneurialism here is reflected in the weighting of UK versus non-UK social entrepreneurs in the book, but we have sought to highlight brilliant examples from around the world.

We write regular blogs and produce a series of podcasts. We will also be organizing a series of events where people will be encouraged to come up with constructive suggestions. We want to stimulate a discussion where ideas come together so that we can develop a coherent system that creates a sustainable and fair world for the future.

This book is just the start. Please be engaged and join in at **www.newismtalks.com**.

Mel Young and Alexandra Matthews
April 2020

Chapter 1

Let’s start with the positivity of social entrepreneurs

Things must change. How many times a day, a week, do we hear those words? People are always expressing their dissatisfaction with their current circumstances, and the state of the world, but how often do we actually do anything?

We are writing this book as the COVID-19 pandemic proliferates around the world, causing lockdowns and economic paralysis. A pandemic has always been high on the global risk register. They have caused widespread death in the past, and it was only a matter of time before another pandemic struck. The 2020 crisis is different to any that has gone before because the world has never been so hyper-connected, both physically and virtually. The virus was able to spread so quickly because of our ability as a species to travel around the world in a matter of hours. And we were able to learn how to protect ourselves by connecting with one another through the internet.

There are two phrases that are used constantly during lockdown: 'when we return to normal' and 'things will be different in the future.'

Many see social protection as the central role of any government at any time and believe it was right for governments to intervene in the way they have done, even if it meant creating a massive overdraft. But many of those same governments are putting out a very clear message: once the pandemic is tamed, then things will return to normal. In other words, they will return to the way they were before. They argue that this is merely a pothole in the road – a large one – but that once it is filled in, we will continue on the same road as before.

There is a contrasting view. Others argue that what has happened has created a profound shift in mindset across society. People's values have shifted: they have become much more respectful of each other. Bonds have been formed between people who have been supporting one another in their own neighbourhoods – many are hopeful that those bonds will remain intact after the virus has left town. People working on the so-called front line – supermarket workers, nurses, waste collectors, care collectors and many more – have been the recipients of profound respect and gratitude. There is a growing feeling that they should be seen as essential workers and paid properly, not as unskilled fodder at the base of the economy food chain. Strong communities are going to emerge based on a different set of values.

It is difficult to predict what will happen. A lot will depend on those who shape the global economy and its underlying principles for the future.

But fundamental change does need to happen. We set up The New Ism in 2018 because we believed – and we still do – that there should be a fundamental shift in how the world operates. Many economists over the years have said that problems in the global economy are leading to huge inequality and that the planet is being destroyed in the relentless pursuit of growth. While many of these economists have put forward suggestions about how to change the direction of the global economy, none have come up with a completely new system. Their suggestions are somehow always tagged to the current economic system.

What we wanted to look at was how to create a completely new system that was based on new thinking. No, we don't have the answers, but we believe that people know intuitively that the current system isn't sustainable. They're just not sure how to change it. That's why so many people have been talking about how this pandemic has given us time to reflect on how we can – and should – come out the other side with a renewed vision for the future. Many say that this vision should be based on the strength of local communities. While that may be true, it is also likely that most people will have to return to the old ways of working and living, as the governments of the world and the global economic architects reboot the economy of the 'normal.' All the goodwill that has built up over the course of the pandemic could evaporate quickly as we go back to focusing on surviving in the old model.

This is the first in a series of books that will examine what a New Ism will look like in the future. As we said, we don't have the answers right now, but there are many talented people who have ideas about what the world might look like. There are lots of practical initiatives underway that are impactful and full of hope.

In this first book, we are concentrating on social entrepreneurship. This is a field we have both worked in:

Mel as a social entrepreneur and Alexandra in a variety of roles in the social entrepreneurship space. We believe the practical action that social entrepreneurs across the world are taking could form the basis of an entirely new global system that is both sustainable and fair.

One of the key cornerstones of The New Ism is about being positive. We don't want to continually refer back to the current system. In a sense, we are starting with a blank piece of paper; continual negativity about the current system simply clutters up thinking. In re-imagining how the world might work more effectively, we need not only change the whole picture, but also to remove the picture frame entirely. Social entrepreneurs are wired up in a very constructive way, which is why we are starting with them.

Having said that, it is important to get the negatives out of the way first. We need to examine the main issues that people are unhappy about, the main issues that need to be changed.

It is fair to say that there is a basic contradiction in the modern world. Statistics show that, over the past 70 years, materially, we have become much better off. Global poverty has declined, with China and India showing particularly significant drops. Healthcare throughout the world is much more advanced and effective – even given the challenges posed by COVID-19 – with child mortality rates decreasing. People are living longer, healthier lives. There are fewer wars. Technological advances have allowed us to communicate around the world with ease, and travel to anywhere in the world is now quite straightforward.

Of course, everything is not perfect. Although the number of wars has decreased considerably, there are still wars in which thousands of innocent people are killed, maimed and made homeless. Despite the decreasing level of poverty, caused mainly by the declines in Asia, there is still a significant number of people simply surviving on next to nothing; homelessness persists in every country in the world. The gap between the richest and poorest in society continues to grow. And we still haven't learned how to protect ourselves against pandemics.

But overall, these trends over the last 70 years are all good news, aren't they? However, when you ask people if they are happy, they tend to answer negatively. They talk about declining mental health due to the stresses and strains of our modern way of living. Mental wellbeing, which was never on the agenda for most countries, has quite suddenly become an issue. There is something that people are finding instinctively wrong about the world in which they live.

A lot of that has to do with climate change and what is happening to the environment. Our entire system is based on growth, but the world is finite. We cannot keep growing forever. It is illogical, and people either consciously or subconsciously know that. Something has to change, and that needs to be articulated.

So, in terms of negativity, what are the issues that people want to raise? There are many, but here are the top five: leadership, inequality, governance, community, and climate change and the environment. We explore each of these issues in more detail in the book to provide context as to how we can move on from them, but always in the spirit of being constructive and positive.

Leadership

When you ask people about the areas that concern them, leadership – or, rather, a lack of it – is always mentioned. It is unclear whether people find all types of leadership to be weak, but, when they speak about leadership, they always refer to politicians and politics. It seems that there is a huge distrust of political leadership, and that feeling is practically universal around the globe.

One view is that the main reason for this is that the world's political systems have not developed at the same pace as the world itself. But when you ask the same people who don't trust political leadership what they would do instead, they don't have an answer. There is huge negativity toward political leadership, without any coherent alternative system.

Of course, leadership isn't all about politics. There are global leaders in business and the media who earn respect, but trust isn't necessarily a word associated with them. You can go back in history and create lists of great leaders, or leaders you might admire and respect. Let's pick a few at random from history: Nelson Mandela, Martin Luther King, Jr, Catherine the Great,

Mother Teresa, Julius Caesar, Vladimir Lenin, Mahatma Gandhi. Were they only leaders for their time or would they be relevant for today? Great leaders aren't necessarily good people – they can be evil – so are we still putting too much emphasis on individuals? What does good leadership look like in this modern world?

In these days where media is so dominant in our lives and where the culture of celebrity forms a backbone to this media, we find broadcasters and media personalities taking up leadership roles that can be incredibly influential. This doesn't necessarily correlate with good leadership, but the media in all of its forms influences us massively. To create good leadership, do we need to control the power of the media?

Are there real leaders within our communities already who just aren't recognized? Possibly. The coronavirus pandemic is showing us where leadership really lies in our communities – in hospitals, in care homes and in public service. There are also thousands of social entrepreneurs around the world doing some great work while showing real leadership skills. They certainly command trust and respect. Are they the global leaders of the future?

What does good leadership look like in this modern world?

Inequality

Inequality is another deep-rooted issue that is deeply unsettling for many. It seems to many that the current system allows the rich to get richer while leaving the poor to languish on the fringes of society. The gap between those who have and those who have not continues to grow at an alarming rate. It seems that if you have money you can increase your wealth while, if you don't, you simply can't.

There is pushback against what people perceive to be – rightly or wrongly – the huge power wielded by global corporate businesses, which not only seem to make massive amounts of money but do everything they can to avoid paying any taxes. Of course, these companies will respond by saying that they create a huge number of jobs and have sophisticated corporate social responsibility (CSR) policies that help the most vulnerable in society and protect the environment. But people are suspicious, believing that these policies are simply a whitewash for dubious practices. Indeed, there is a feeling that these corporate giants have created a new type of serf economy where workers have low pay and little, if any, job security.

There is a connected issue about regulations and rules. Big businesses are keen to have as few regulations as possible so they can encourage enterprise and growth. While governments maintain that there must be some order to protect their citizens, they are also dependent on the income they receive as taxes from these corporations. This is an awkward balance.

Again, while people feel strongly about this and understand that the economy must be a key part of any fair society, they don't have any concrete suggestions for a new economy that isn't just an update of the current one.

Governance

There is a complex relationship between the government, businesses and the way the economy is controlled, but people are generally negative about governance and distrustful of the state. One of the challenges here is to understand what good governance really means.

In the UK, for example, there are community councils, local governments, regional governments in some cases, and the national government. There is a huge amount of consultation. At national and local levels, the government is always putting plans and much more out for consultation in the wider community. There are all sorts of ways in which people can give their input and yet there is a very strong feeling among the population that they are not listened to. The turnout in the 2018 local elections in England was around 35%[1] – that means that the majority of people don't have their voices heard. Is that because they feel powerless anyway?

There are steadfast rules regarding how businesses should be run. Filing accounts within very clear guidelines is the law of the land and businesses take advice from professional accountants, lawyers and nonexecutive directors to make sure that everything is done properly. Charities are in a similar position and are all closely regulated.

Some directors and trustees will argue that they are overregulated and that there is too much bureaucracy. However, people still don't feel they trust businesses despite this level of scrutiny, even if well-respected external auditors are involved. So, on the one hand you have businesses saying that the administrative burden that is in place for reasons of good governance is too high, while ordinary people still argue that businesses are untrustworthy.

This lack of trust in government and business governance is a real issue for many people. It is caused by a lack of confidence in systems that are often broken and aren't relevant to the needs of communities and individuals. We have already mentioned the lack of trust in government leadership, but are the systems of accounting and associated legal frameworks also no longer fit for the modern world? And if that is the case, what replaces them?

Community

Many people talk about how communities are being destroyed. They have a perspective that communities were much stronger in the past and the pace of modern life has adversely affected where they live. Another repeated phrase is: "We used to know everyone who lived around here, and now we know no one."

There seems to be a collective harking back to a time when there was such a thing as community, although that might be a false memory. The main gripe that people have is that there seems to be an imbalance between the local and the global worlds, the latter of which seems all-controlling. There is an issue about identity – people want to be very clear about where they belong, while at the same time reaping the benefits of being a global citizen (e.g., connectivity, travel and food). There are huge tensions in this part of the discussion and any new system will have to work out how to get this balance right, but it certainly is an area where people currently feel uncomfortable and insecure.

Climate change and the environment

Without a doubt, the biggest challenge and possibly central issue to all of this is about what we are doing to the planet. Are we destroying it to a point where there is no return and no matter what we do, there is no turning back? Younger people, in particular, are deeply concerned about this.

Once again, people are very good at articulating their concerns but not so good at coming up with solutions – solutions that must be sustainable, fair and inclusive. One of the biggest challenges is around an economic system that has growth at its core. How can we create a system that isn't based on growth? Does this mean that we will all have to survive on less? And if so, are we all prepared to make sacrifices in order to create that sustainable economy? It is difficult to give things up. It is difficult to go back in time. If we all agree to travel less, particularly by air, in order to save the planet, will we really stop going on holiday to other parts of the world? Are we really up for relegating exotic holidays to wistful memories?

We also need to consider the impact that reducing travel would have on the economy. We are all on a moral merry-go-round, where we have been convinced that all our actions are positive. We need to get off that merry-go-round before it spins out of control. Once we are off, we need to take stock and look at a new way of living. We need to come up with practical answers. Yes, hold demonstrations about climate change if you like, but the bigger challenge is to come up with constructive suggestions about how to create a sustainable way forward.

Conclusion

The New Ism will turn away from the negativity and the moaning, and toward a can-do attitude of positivity. In this first book, we start with the social entrepreneurs, the alchemists who are already changing the way we think and providing some leadership about how to create a fairer world. It is the right place for us to start. We will start the discussion now and build from here. Please join us: we want to hear your constructive suggestions.

Chapter 2

What exactly is a social entrepreneur?

This chapter is written by Mel Young, drawing from his own experience as a social entrepreneur.

What exactly is a social entrepreneur? It is a very good question. And I want to help you understand.

To me, a social entrepreneur is very similar to a traditional entrepreneur. The big difference between the two is the motivation and outcome. An entrepreneur is typically driven by making money and the excitement of a good idea, whereas a social entrepreneur's motivation is rooted in changing the world for the better, particularly in the areas of social and environmental enhancement.

Entrepreneurs and social entrepreneurs display very similar characteristics. They are driven and don't take no for an answer. They are ambitious, hard-working and see angles where others don't. They make personal sacrifices to achieve their goals, and they will go to the ends of the Earth to achieve those goals. They will take risks, and they certainly aren't nine-to-five people.

But they aren't perfect. They are often obstinate and refuse to budge from their position, on the one hand, while on the other they will suddenly change direction completely. They are often only mediocre managers and can be very difficult to work with. They are completely focused on their goal, and they are open to different angles to hit their objectives.

Entrepreneurs are a defined subset of the business sector. Social entrepreneurs straddle the business and charity sectors and are starting to emerge as a clearly defined group of people with particular characteristics. They understand business models and will use them to achieve sustainable outcomes for wider society. They also believe in the values that underpin charities and will combine them with sustainable business planning to achieve substantial positive impact for society.

The biggest difference between entrepreneurs and social entrepreneurs is the outcome. Social entrepreneurs are solely focused on changing society for the better and, as a breed, they have now been recognized as creators who add value and as leaders.

There are differing definitions of social entrepreneurship. The notion of an entrepreneur is more clearly understood than for the social entrepreneur, which only came into use around the start of this century, so is still a relatively new concept. Consequently, there are numerous definitions that relate to different countries or cultures, which in turn have different legal systems. This isn't an academic book that will explore the different definitions and the different positions that people will take – it's very easy to explore these things online.

Social entrepreneurs are not defined by whatever legal entity they might run. A number of them create hybrid models to carry out their work in the most effective way. While issues of governance and control are important, the real imperative for social entrepreneurs is to change the world, and so they will solely focus on impact and outcome and will use any legal model necessary to achieve that.

I am a social entrepreneur, and I'd like to share my journey with you.

It was in 1997 when someone said to me, "You are a social entrepreneur!" I thought about it for a short while and concluded that it summed me up perfectly. I'd tried to define myself for most of my life without success and suddenly here was the answer. I no longer had an identity crisis.

Up until 1993, I'd gained experience in various aspects that make up the social entrepreneur. I set up a magazine after I left university (the entrepreneur part) and worked in a large housing scheme (the social part). I'd always worked with people, established teams and created opportunities for the people involved.

In 1993, I set up *The Big Issue in Scotland* along with a friend, Tricia Hughes. We both found the level of homelessness and poverty in Scotland at the time abhorrent, and we wanted to do something tangible. *The Big Issue* provided a simple route out of homelessness, and we both bought into the philosophy of 'a hand up rather than a handout,' which, of course, appealed to the social entrepreneurs: social entrepreneurialism is about sustainable, lasting change, not short-term fixes.

The Big Issue was originally founded in the UK in 1991 by John Bird (now Lord John Bird) and Gordon Roddick, the co-founder of The Body Shop. Both men were from different backgrounds, but they were incredibly entrepreneurial, and *The Big Issue* was a huge success. Tricia and I spoke to them about bringing the magazine up from London to Scotland, but their focus at the time was on London's severe homelessness problem, so we established a completely separate organization in Scotland and signed an agreement to use *The Big Issue* name. It was a type of franchise; maybe it was the first-ever social franchise.

The Big Issue in Scotland was a resounding success. Not only did it impact the lives of many homeless people in a very positive way, it also changed the whole profile of social enterprise and challenged the traditional notion of charity as the only solution to social problems.

To do justice to the story of *The Big Issue* would take another book. Suffice to say that it was a very special time, that created an explosion in entrepreneurial thinking. The Scottish social enterprise created a number of ventures, including a bank and a recycling unit, as well as helping develop the street newspaper concept across the world, particularly in Russia and former Eastern bloc countries. *The Big Issue in Scotland* and the original *The Big Issue* merged in 2003.

What was fascinating to some people at the time was that we had emerged from nowhere and all of a sudden we were on everyone's lips. There were many reasons, but the key component was the innovative drive from social entrepreneurs. A can-do culture had emerged, and new ideas were welcomed. They didn't all work, but energy levels were high. Another key factor was that *The Big Issue in Scotland* was financially self-sufficient from the start. It did not have to rely on grants or handouts, which can often slow progress or create mission drift. This gave it the oxygen it needed to develop at speed. In the early years, it was like being on an express train – crazy at times for sure, but ultimately very satisfying because the positive impact on human life was substantial.

In the 1990s, the social enterprise sector started to emerge. This was more about the legal entity than the purpose – the middle ground between a business and charity – but support for the concept was growing.

In many ways, the idea of a social enterprise isn't so new: lots of people claim that they came up with the concept. But traditional business has always grappled with its role in society. Of course, many businesses made their owners very wealthy as they exploited poorly paid workers (sadly, that is still the case in many places across the world), but there has always been an alternative view to the role of business. One of the most famous is Robert Owen, who owned a large textile mill based in New Lanark in central Scotland around the beginning of 1800. Owen paid all his workers well and provided a supportive community for everyone connected with the mill. His philosophy was anti-exploitative, but he also understood that productivity increased when you had a healthy, happy and well-educated workforce.

Owen was ahead of his time, but a lot of his thinking is applied by many modern businesses, which see that there is a role beyond simply making a profit. The Body Shop is a great example. Its founders,

Gordon and Anita Roddick, understood the notion of profit and purpose going hand in hand and built a hugely successful business around an incredibly effective environmental campaign.

I remember attending a meeting they helped organize in Prague in the mid-1990s. They were part of a fascinating organization called Social Venture Network (SVN), which had been established in 1987. While I had been involved in a successful social enterprise in Scotland, I had no idea of the breadth and scale of the interventions that were happening around the world. There were many businesses in attendance, discussing how they could be a force for good, but there were also many others that were using business models to create social or environmental good. This was my first interface with social entrepreneurs – although I didn't call them that at the time – from all over the world. Some of these people were the pioneers behind concepts such as fair trade or microfinance, and they not only shared what they were doing but explained how they were going to scale and how the world would change.

It was exhilarating, and I felt that anything was possible. The connection and energy between these like-minded people was electric. It was around this point that someone said the magical words: "You are a social entrepreneur," and, suddenly, I knew who I was!

In 1998, I helped establish a network organization called Senscot (Social Entrepreneurs Scotland) that was, very simply, a network to support those people who saw themselves as social entrepreneurs or ran organizations as social enterprises. I was also beginning to discover more about people who were identified as social entrepreneurs around the world.

In 2001, I was invited to become a Fellow of the Schwab Foundation for Social Entrepreneurs, which had very recently been established by Klaus and Hilde Schwab in Switzerland to support social entrepreneurs. I was one of an inaugural group of 30 that convened in Geneva to meet each other and hear about the foundation's vision.

Klaus Schwab is the President and Founder of the World Economic Forum. To have that organization identify social entrepreneurs as a clearly defined group with a particular DNA, and to give it an identity, really helped our credibility as individuals. It also helped put the concept of social entrepreneurship much further up the agenda. The social entrepreneurs appointed in 2001 were invited to join the 2002 annual meeting of the World Economic Forum, which is held each year in Davos, Switzerland.

This allowed social entrepreneurs to interact with some of the world's key influencers from business, government and the media; just as importantly, it allowed social entrepreneurs to get to know one another. What was abundantly clear was that, despite the very different causes these social entrepreneurs were involved in and the diverse geography, they had exactly the same DNA – that drive and passion, that never-say-die attitude and that determination to make the world a better place.

We shared our successes as well as our challenges and failures. We connected at a deep level and many of us became close friends. It was the birth of a unique family.

Despite the significant intervention of the Schwab Foundation, the notion of social entrepreneurship had been around for a while. One of the first people to identify the sector was Bill Drayton, who saw what was going on when he was working as a management consultant at McKinsey. He established a highly respected global network called Ashoka in 1980. He believed that social entrepreneurs were a particular type of person and, as such, they needed support. Ashoka is set up to support individuals rather than organizations. Bill's view is that if the leaders or founders of organizations are supported effectively, then the organizations they are involved in have a much greater chance of success. Ashoka also throws its weight behind the concept of social entrepreneurship. They now have over 3,000 elected Fellows in their network in over 70 countries. I am lucky enough to be one of their Fellows.

Other network organizations have followed. Jeff Skoll, one of the founders of eBay, established the Skoll Foundation, which provides significant support to social entrepreneurs around the world, as well as raising the profile of the whole social entrepreneurship sector.

The biggest difference between entrepreneurs and social entrepreneurs is the outcome. Social entrepreneurs are solely focused on changing society for the better and, as a breed, they have now been recognized as creators and leaders who add value.

Combined together, the impact of social entrepreneurs around the globe has been significant. It is true that the development of these networks for individual social entrepreneurs has helped raise the profile of social entrepreneurship, but the sector continues to develop. While the individual social entrepreneurs in these networks have been given a platform, giving them credibility and a profile, there are thousands of social entrepreneurs quietly getting on with their work and making a positive intervention in their communities around the world. You don't necessarily need global recognition to be an effective social entrepreneur.

This is a point made by Lawrence Demarco, one of the founders of Senscot. While he recognizes the key role that founders and leaders play in the setting up and development of any enterprise, he believes the long-term impact and sustainability of the organization is more important than any one individual. He is a passionate believer in the need to build sustainable local communities in this modern world. He believes that genuine local communities must be the cornerstone of any modern economy and that, while social entrepreneurs have a vital role in building those communities, they aren't the only players. He is uncomfortable with what might be termed the 'celebrity culture' around social entrepreneurship and how an obsession with those individuals actually detracts from the positive impact that can be made by the development of local communities.

This is an interesting observation because he is worried that social entrepreneurs are lulled into a mirror image of what is wrong in the world: celebrity and a fixation on growth. It is the same issue as the discussion around scale. I remember in the early days of the Schwab Foundation, I had a discussion with Martha (Pati) Ruiz Corzo, who runs a very special environmental programme in Sierra Gorda in Mexico. At the time, many of the social entrepreneurs were focused on scale and the growth of their organizations. I was in that camp. By then, I had started the Homeless World Cup, an annual football tournament that uses football as a tool to help homeless people help themselves – you can read more about it in Chapter 6. I could see the potential for considerable impact around the world. We could potentially change the lives of thousands of homeless people. I was enthusiastic and probably obsessed with the vision, but Martha brought me up short. When I asked her about her plans to grow and develop in other countries, she told me clearly that she didn't have any. She would concentrate on improving the depth and quality of her organization locally. Full stop. I remember being initially taken aback by this but, on reflection, it made sense.

Laurence Demarco is right, in a sense: as this sector is still in its early days, it is easy to get swept along as if we are champions. What we have created with the Homeless World Cup does work as a global initiative and we are right to go to scale and plan for growth, because we know that the impact will be substantial. But Martha is also right because what she wants to do is build something of quality that is sustainable in her own region. People can visit it and be inspired to do something similar on their own – and they do – but global growth isn't on her agenda.

It is possible for social entrepreneurs to sit down together and have different mindsets and be incredibly impactful in their own ways. We have similar DNA, and we don't have to be swept along by a model that is all about growth; this is the point that Lawrence and Martha make. But we will inspire and openly support one another.

The Schwab Foundation has recently changed the criteria for its Fellowship, moving it away from being solely for social entrepreneurs to include those who are being entrepreneurial in a social sense within their own arena of work, whether that's government, business, academia or the arts. The message is that, in order to create real change, we need to have social innovators across all sections of society. Social entrepreneurs who are pioneering at the coalface are one thing, but having others working within established institutions can create significant impact too. Sometimes these people are referred to as 'intrapreneurs'; despite being very influential and doing important work, they are usually completely under the radar.

The trick here is to identify the 'intrapreneurs' and connect them with the entrepreneurs and then let some magic happen! Social entrepreneurs can often become isolated on the front line, but, by forging links with institutions, there is an opportunity to create effective interventions. This is the belief behind the change of direction from the Schwab Foundation. Critics have argued that this move waters down the definition of social entrepreneurship. They believe that social entrepreneurs are a distinct breed and that, by creating a clear definition, it helps provide them with a proper identity, which in turn leads to the potential of greater support.

This discussion will go on because the sector is still not clearly formed, but there is clear momentum, as the desire to organize the world in a different way gathers some pace.

I am older now, although I still feel young and have lots of energy. With my fellow social entrepreneurs Andrea Coleman and Chris Underhill, I have co-founded a new organization called Elders for Social Entrepreneurs, which will provide a space for those social entrepreneurs coming to the end of their careers. We don't use the word 'retire' because that simply isn't in the DNA of most social entrepreneurs. We can never imagine any social entrepreneur putting their feet up and drifting into old age, but we established the organization because social entrepreneurs almost always put their work and their impact before themselves. They are so embroiled in achieving their objectives that they don't look at issues like exit planning, board development, succession, pension planning and so on.

This new entity will provide a place where these issues can be discussed, and individuals can be given support and mentorship. This advice will also be available to younger social entrepreneurs, who should be thinking about these types of issues at a much earlier stage. To many new social entrepreneurs who are starting out with zeal and determination, the thought of discussing exit planning at such an early stage will seem like a contradiction, but this whole area has been neglected and should become part of the long-term planning process.

One area that is never discussed is mergers. Social entrepreneurs are brilliant at setting up and growing their organizations, but it is their life's work and can be very difficult to let go. One possible exit plan is to merge with other social enterprises or think through an effective succession plan with other social entrepreneurs. Another new organization, called Catalyst 2030, is dedicated to pulling social entrepreneurs together to create genuine systems change. It will be interesting to see how effective social entrepreneurs can be when they collaborate.

Conclusion

While the definitions may be blurred and the academics debate the real meaning, I know what I am. I am a social entrepreneur. I can't help it; it's what I am, it's my default position. Other social entrepreneurs will know exactly what I mean. The world is facing some significant challenges and people are looking for change, but, more than that, they are looking for a change that creates genuine sustainability and wellbeing. Social entrepreneurs are the alchemists who can work with others to help build an inclusive and fair world.

Chapter 3

Just who are these social entrepreneurs?

This chapter is written by Mel Young, drawing from his own experience as a social entrepreneur.

There is always a debate about how much support you give to the leading global social entrepreneurs, as opposed to those who operate under the radar at a smaller community level. To me, the answer is simple: you support both. In many ways, an unknown social entrepreneur can be as impactful in the local community as a high-profile social entrepreneur who operates globally. You can be inspired by anyone.

In a sense, they are all the same. They have the same DNA and the same passion to change society. I'd like to share some of the people I have met along the way who have inspired me. They are not in any order, and there are many other inspirational people who I have not mentioned. I have met hundreds of social entrepreneurs on my journey, and they all have been inspirational. Here are a few.

I must mention Muhammad Yunus. I had read a lot about him and his work in Bangladesh, and I was fascinated by the practical impact he was making through his microfinance scheme, Grameen Bank, which was lifting thousands of people out of poverty. Furthermore, and even more incredibly, his simple concept of microbanking aimed solely at poor people was being replicated by other people in different parts of the world. You can read more about Muhammad's work in Chapter 8.

So, I was thrilled to meet him in Geneva in 2001. We were attending the same conference, where he was speaking. I wanted to write an article about him for a magazine in the UK, but I knew he would be very short of time and indeed there were many people queuing up to speak with him. I asked him meekly if he had any time for an interview.

I'll never forget his reply. "I have all the time in the world," he said.

I expected he would be able to spare ten minutes, but we ended up talking for over an hour. I remember thinking, "Here is a man who can expand time." He made time elastic! He was very keen to share his experiences and insights and was one of those people who had an ability to make it seem as if you were the only other person in the world.

He was clearly very intelligent and, although his concept is simple, there is very smart thinking behind the work he was doing. He displayed all those human traits that you find in most social entrepreneurs: he was humble, but he was also very clear about his purpose, and he had a steely determination to achieve his vision. And all of that was based on a set of guiding values, on which his microfinance operations and subsequent global projects were built. Those human qualities shine through social entrepreneurs because their work is focused on higher outcomes rather than selfish gains.

Jeroo Billimoria is another serial social entrepreneur. She is the founder of Childline in India, which she set up to provide a lifeline for street children in India. You can read more about her work with Childline in Chapter 7. Following the success of Childline and not willing to rest on her laurels, Jeroo created new enterprises

– Child and Youth Finance International and Aflatoun International. Both organizations operate around the globe and have impacted the lives of millions of children and youth by providing them with financial help and advice. Jeroo is now based in Amsterdam and, of course, keeps coming up with new ventures. She has established the One Family Foundation to help support new social enterprises and is one of the leading lights behind Catalyst 2030, which is designed to bring the social entrepreneurial sector together to create genuine system change across the globe.

Please listen to Jeroo speaking if you get the chance. Positivity pours out of her. She exudes contagious energy. I remember when I first met her, and we were listening to a rather dry academic presentation. She passed me a note that said simply, "I'm bored." I wanted to burst out laughing but managed to suppress it, and I passed her a note back saying, "So am I." I think there is a bit of devilment or delinquency in all social entrepreneurs. Don't ask us to sit in a row and take notes, because we simply won't conform. We aren't particularly good at taking instruction, but we are very quick to grasp concepts and apply them appropriately; that will always require a bit of magical delinquency.

Jeroo is able to turn concepts into scalable activity quickly and impact the lives of many people. She does this by being able to look at things in a different way. Social entrepreneurs don't dismiss anything out of hand, but they don't just accept what they are told.

In many ways, an unknown social entrepreneur can be as impactful in the local community as a high-profile social entrepreneur who operates globally.

Is Jimmy Wales, the founder of Wikipedia, a social entrepreneur? He is defined in many different ways, for sure, most notably as a technology pioneer, but for me he is a social entrepreneur to the core.

I met him years ago, and I was very struck by his deep understanding of the power and use of online technology as a force for good or bad. When I talked to him, the online giants like Facebook and Google were exploding into our consciousness, destined, as we now know, to make unfathomable amounts of money. Jimmy explained to me – in simple terms because technology usually baffles me – that there were two potential routes to creating something like Wikipedia: one for open source and one using traditional business models.

Wikipedia is simply an online encyclopaedia created by its users. It is a not-for-profit organization that is funded through supportive donations. It could have been created in a different way. The idea of having an online encyclopaedia is a smart one; somewhere you can get information about anything at the press of a button. In the business route, the site would be full of adverts, promotions and paywalls; the founders could have made a fortune. But Jimmy created an online service that is totally free to all. The beauty of this is that it has created huge customer loyalty. It would be very difficult for someone to create a viable alternative that made them lots of money. Wikipedia is the people's encyclopaedia, and it is here to stay.

Is that being a social entrepreneur? Jimmy has used his technical nous and business acumen to create something that is viable, useful and free to use, despite having the option to go down another path. His legacy is a very valuable asset, which is accessible by everyone at no cost. That's being a very smart social entrepreneur.

Rodrigo Baggio is another social entrepreneur who uses technology in an impactful way. He was another of the first cohort of social entrepreneurs who joined the Schwab Foundation in 2001, which is how I met him. He is based in Brazil, where he founded and runs the Centre for Digital Inclusion (CDI), which he established to bridge the wide digital divide in his country. He targets underserved communities, particularly young people and those who are excluded. He provides free hardware, such as computers, and has created centres across the country. His unique proposition is the programmes for shared solutions that he has developed, where young people are given the use of technology and then asked to come up with solutions to the challenges faced by their own communities. His unique way of working has given rise to startling and impactful results.

There has been a lot written about how technology or online platforms can be used to tackle some of the world's most intractable problems. I think there is a truth in this, but it isn't the be-all and end-all. Some people believe they can become social entrepreneurs simply by setting up a tech business and sitting in a bedroom somewhere. That is hogwash. It is the interaction

Social entrepreneurs may well be characterized by their humility, but they all have fire in their bellies.

with people that creates genuine outcomes. Rodrigo is an inspiration in this regard. By using technology, he is educating thousands of young people who are excluded from the system. His impact is substantial.

Vera Cordeiro is also from Brazil, where she trained as a doctor. She is a committed social entrepreneur who has been recognized for her work in the health sector, where she has used her skills and invention to change the way health is delivered to the poorest families in Brazil. At last count, she had created 23 non-governmental organizations (NGOs) around hospitals based on Associação Saúde Criança, the organization she founded in 1991. Her concept has been copied and applied in other countries around the world. In her case, of course, she will use technology, but it is the face-to-face interaction combined with her innovation and her kindness that makes her organizations so successful.

Sir Fazle Abed was the founder of BRAC, which creates opportunities for people living in poverty. Sadly, he died in 2019 at the age of 83. He was busy being a successful social entrepreneur in Bangladesh long before the term was even coined. He started his career as a successful accountant at a large company, but gave up his position to serve the poor. He established BRAC in 1972, harnessing business principles to build his organization and change people's lives through the central philosophy of a hand up, rather than a handout (identical to the founding principle of *The Big Issue*).

He fought the belief that there would always be poor people in any society and believed passionately that, given the right tools, even the poorest of the poor would find a way out of poverty.

By the time of Fazle's death, BRAC employed 30,000 people in Bangladesh and had intervened in every aspect of life in the country, lifting many thousands out of poverty. His organization employs many people in other countries around the world as it continues to change people's lives. It is the biggest social enterprise in the world by some considerable distance.

Just like many other social entrepreneurs, Fazle was an unassuming and humble man. He was always clear in his views. I remember a time when we were in a discussion with other social entrepreneurs from around the world about ownership and scale. We were talking about succession planning and how we built trust into the governance of our respective organizations so that they did not drift away from their founding principles.

Fazel said that his organization was in some ways a conglomerate of smaller enterprises, and he had simply brought his extended family in to run key parts. Social entrepreneurs from the Western world were shocked and said that this wouldn't be countenanced in their countries because nepotism was seriously frowned upon, particularly in the charitable sector.

He couldn't understand it. He saw his organization in many ways as a family business: surely your family were the people you would trust with something that you had spent your whole life building. "Why," he asked, "would you bring complete strangers onto your boards, even if they have smart degrees and lots of money?" He believed it didn't make any sense at all.

His thoughts kicked off a great discussion around how trust is created in any organization and the role of the founding social entrepreneur and longer-term sustainability. Sure, there were cultural differences between Bangladesh and the West, but we were all grappling with the same issue: how to build transparent, successful social organizations that would survive and be impactful in the years to come. His wisdom and insights during that discussion were invaluable, but the gentle way he introduced the subject, which then sparked sometimes fierce debate, was equally smart. He will always be known as one of the world's leading social entrepreneurs.

Social entrepreneurs may well be characterized by their humility, but they all have fire in their bellies. None more so than Martin Burt, who is the founder Fundación Paraguaya in Paraguay, which is dedicated to promoting equality through microfinance and financial literacy, particularly for young people. Martin has also established a number of different organizations and sits on the boards of global international networks. He speaks eloquently and well about the need to end poverty by bringing together the stories of suffering from individual families and connecting that to a wider macro-economic global picture, which he believes must change if the micro-economic interventions have any chance of making the desired impact. Once again, you cannot fail to be drawn to him through his absolute passion and desire to end global poverty.

I have mentioned seven well-known social entrepreneurs whose stories are all inspiring. And that's just seven out of many more stories about individual social entrepreneurs who are just as inspiring in their own way. Some are great friends I could easily mention, but I want to finish this chapter in a different way.

In Scotland, where I live, there have been a number of community buy-outs. In some cases, the community has bought land from absentee landlords and the result has been a transformation in these areas. Where there once was serious de-population, now islands and other areas have been brought back to life by communities that have obtained the assets and transformed them into sustainable places to live. The Scottish government has now brought in legislation that makes it much easier for communities to purchase land and assets.

It is a good-news story all round. Land that was lying fallow and falling into disrepair has been transformed. My question is, can any of us name any of the people who were behind this innovative community approach? They must have shown all the attributes of social entrepreneurs. They had to come up with a vision, raise capital and work hard to transform places, all of which has had a substantial impact both for the society locally and for the environment. It is a huge success story – it has everything in it, but no one can answer my question.

The reason is that the people behind this were working for a common cause and working as a team. Yes, they were happy to be quoted in the media when and if necessary, but they didn't seek praise, and they didn't want to be catapulted onto a bigger stage. And yet, their interventions have been very significant.

Conclusion

There are social entrepreneurs everywhere. Some have big profiles while others have none, but their impact is significant no matter what. There will be a social entrepreneur near you, and they will be making a difference. As the world tries to recover from the global coronavirus pandemic, working out how to organize daily life differently and how to prioritize different values, social entrepreneurs will have an ever-increasing role to play as leaders. You have an opportunity to support them or even become one yourself.

Chapter 4

How to become a social entrepreneur

This chapter is written by Mel Young, drawing from his own experience as a social entrepreneur.

A lot of people ask me how they can become a social entrepreneur. Well, you don't have to ask permission; it isn't a club.

There has been plenty written about that age-old question: are entrepreneurs born or are they made? Academic courses have been prepared and books written on this subject without any clear answer. We think there are two answers, and both are correct: you can be born to be an entrepreneur, but you can also learn to be one. Everyone's circumstances are different. What drives people is different. And sometimes entrepreneurial zeal appears when you don't expect it.

My stock answer to anyone who asks me how to become a social entrepreneur is that, before anything else, you must have real passion and drive to do something – that's essential – and then just do it.

As the concept of social entrepreneurship has emerged, it has attracted a lot of attention and even become quite trendy. This helps attract people to the sector, which is good news, but any successful social entrepreneur who we have come across – no matter if they are operating locally or internationally – have all been driven by a fundamental desire to create real change.

This desire or passion is an essential ingredient if you want to become a social entrepreneur. It is possible to come up with a smart idea, but unless you are prepared to throw your life at your venture with passion and belief, you will have much less chance of success.

Motivation is less important than passion and desire. We know people who have been born into poverty and their reason for becoming a social entrepreneur is that they are determined to change the circumstances of people who might fall into poverty as they did. But we know other people who have never lived in poverty but who see a world that is full of inequality and are determined to do something about it. Both have made superb social entrepreneurs.

Similarly, we know people who weren't particularly aware of environmental issues but were horrified when trees were cut down in their local neighbourhood and created an environmental social enterprise in response. Increased knowledge around the wider environmental issues followed and the social enterprise grew accordingly, with positive results.

People are motivated in all sorts of ways and at all sorts of times. Bart Weejens, a Dutch social entrepreneur, loved rats when he was a boy and came to understand their extensive positive assets. He believed that they would be very efficient at detecting land mines and could be trained to locate them. Initially people laughed at him, but he persisted and demonstrated that they were much more efficient than other animals, including dogs, which were being used extensively. He established his organization, APOPO, created what he called HeroRat technology and, slowly but surely, started to be taken seriously as the rats proved how efficient they were at finding mines.

APOPO has grown, and the rats are now also trained to detect diseases such as tuberculosis. Bart has received a lot of recognition for his work and the associated smart technology, which has saved many lives as a result of land mine clearing and detecting illnesses. It was his drive and passion, particularly in those early days, which have made those outcomes possible.

Another key attribute that successful social entrepreneurs demonstrate is their ability to unite people around their cause, even from a very early stage. Yes, they may have bucketloads of passion, but that won't help build an impactful organization or movement unless they can bring other people with them on the journey. From the start, social entrepreneurs need to be looking out for people who share their passion and can be persuaded to join in. You must identify the skills you need to build the movement; equally, you need to be honest with yourself about what skills you have and don't have.

Many successful social entrepreneurs will describe the early days of their venture as being part of a family or part of a team where everyone rolled their sleeves up in order to achieve initial objectives. The atmosphere is always one of collaboration with a real spirit of determination, and a sense of pride when targets are achieved. Getting that culture right in the early days is crucial. Everyone must buy into the initial vision and then feel that they 'own' it.

I started the Homeless World Cup with my friend and colleague Harald Schmidt, who ran a street paper called *Das Megaphon* in Graz in Austria. We were both very committed to the idea. Yes, a lot of people said that we were crazy – even people who knew us well thought that our idea would never work. But we were determined, and we wouldn't take no for an answer. But we couldn't do it all on our own. We needed a broad team of people to back what we were doing.

We needed experts in football, sponsorship, event organization and communications. Of course, by 2001, when we came up with the idea, we both had a lot of experience of working with homeless people, but we had to bring in partners globally who were working with homeless people in their own countries on a day-to-day basis. Without these people, the Homeless World Cup simply wouldn't exist.

We were building a movement and, in some senses, a large part of our work in those early days was as salespeople. We were selling a concept or an idea that to many people was crazy, so it wasn't easy. But we kept working on it and slowly the movement began to grow; by 2002, some key people began to back us.

So social entrepreneurs must have passion, but they also must have determination. It was hard convincing people to support the Homeless World Cup in those early days, but we never gave up, despite some setbacks. In one case, a sponsor who agreed to support us pulled out and left us in a very difficult position. But we carried on and the first Homeless World Cup took place in Graz in Austria in 2003; it was a huge success.

Motivation is less important than passion and desire.

We were only going to have one event but research feedback into the impact of the event, particularly for homeless people, was very positive, so we decided to develop and grow the organization. As a result, 1.2 million homeless people in more than 70 countries have benefited. It continues to be a huge success but those three ingredients – passion, determination and an effective team – are ever-present, and I am convinced that they form the basis of how to be a successful social entrepreneur.

I believe that there is some truth in the expression, 'build it and they will come.' People generally don't like inequality. Since I started working with homeless people back in 1993, I have given many talks to a wide range of people, from young school children right through to some of the wealthiest and most powerful people in the world. At some point during each talk I ask, "Does anyone think homelessness is a good idea?" No one in all those years has said yes. My response is simple: why do we have it then? People are generally very sympathetic to the cause that social entrepreneurs lead, be it in the social or environmental space, because instinctively they understand the situation but feel impotent to do anything about it. People will therefore warm to an impactful concept. Build it and they will come.

Sometimes when people ask me about becoming a social entrepreneur; they expect me to talk about the correct legal entity and accounting procedures.

Obviously, these areas are important, but they shouldn't be the first consideration. Feel the passion first and don't be too inhibited by the organizational niceties at the beginning; they will follow naturally and there is plenty of good organizational advice available these days for budding social entrepreneurs to digest. It is that inner belief social entrepreneurs have – allied with a world view among the wider population that 'something needs to change' – that will make ventures a success because people will indeed come!

Apart from being good at sales, successful social entrepreneurs are very good storytellers. This is directly connected to their inner passion. Ask any successful social entrepreneur about what they do, and they will articulate it very well and with feeling, combining relevant data with human interest stories. It is a compelling mix that is digestible in a modern world inundated with media messages every second. It is so important for social entrepreneurs to build an effective brand that includes all the positive aspects of their work. That brand and how it is marketed will form an important part of the overall planning. I believe that storytelling is a vital part of the armoury of social entrepreneurs. They have great stories to tell, and people are genuinely interested.

Of course, while I go on about passion, determination and team creation as the key ingredients, it is important to create the right plan, just like in any venture. Planning is a fundamental part of any business concern and social entrepreneurs need to pay attention to the detail of this at an early stage. Some would argue that social entrepreneurs are 'big picture' people rather than 'detail' people, and I think that is largely true. But one of the main attributes of social entrepreneurs is that they are aware of their weaknesses and can bring in people who are good with the intricacies of running a business.

There are three crucial components to this.

Storytelling is a vital part of the armoury of social entrepreneurs.

1. Setting up the appropriate legal entity

I don't believe that there is one legal entity that is appropriate for social entrepreneurs around the globe. If there were, it would be an easy recommendation to make. The challenge is all about creating a legal entity that combines business disciplines with charitable outcomes. There have been attempts in many countries to create something that captures the idea; they all have positives and negatives, which is why you'll find social entrepreneurs sometimes doing similar work but through different legal entities. For social entrepreneurs, the priority is their vision, and that's about changing the world.

The establishment of B Corporations is an attempt to combine both worlds, and it goes some way to doing this. However, some people don't believe it captures the essence of genuine social entrepreneurship and shy away from it. Other entities include social business, nonprofit social enterprises, for-profit social enterprises and community interest companies. Some people have strong views about this: they don't believe anybody should be benefiting from a social organization and that profits should be forbidden, whereas others believe the complete opposite.

In some cases, this is driven by the culture of the country where the legal body operates. In the US, many are quite comfortable with the concept of a for-profit social enterprise, whereas in the UK the opposite is true. This might stem from the fact that there are bodies providing government services under a public sector contract that call themselves social enterprises. The criticism is that, while these might be efficient, well-run companies, they are not really enterprising or adding any social value.

Then, of course, there are charities, the concept of which is understood throughout the world. Money is raised and used for a good cause. Critics argue that charities foster a culture of dependency or fulfil roles that should be undertaken by the state. Social entrepreneurs simply use charities as a vehicle to achieve their aims.

There is no perfect vehicle and many social entrepreneurs create 'hybrids,' which might contain two or three different entities that work together to focus on one outcome. An example might be a for-profit limited company that channels its profits into the not-for-profit branch, thereby providing a reliable income stream and negating the need to be reliant on grants.

For Alex and me, there is no right or wrong answer. The only issue is the outcome of the organization, which must be positive for the whole of society. Getting the correct legal entity sorted at the outset is important and there is plenty of advice now available in most countries. Don't let the muddied water put you off; your vision and passion are more important. Settle on the legal entity that feels most comfortable for you and then knock 'em dead.

2. Getting the right board

As the legal entity is set up, getting the right people onto your board is vital. The makeup of boards will differ according to the organization's specific needs, but directors must support the founding social entrepreneur. It is important to set up the ownership structure and the lines of control from the outset. The role of the non-executive director also needs to be clarified, again from the beginning.

Too often, well-meaning non-executive directors inhibit or completely demotivate the founding social entrepreneur. This is where the type of legal entity becomes important. It is sometimes the case that, in charities, too much power rests with the trustees: this type of entity works well where the organization is large and well established, but might not be appropriate for a social venture, particularly in its start-up period. Social entrepreneurs, like business entrepreneurs, will take risks, and they need the right legal entity and board behind them in order for the entrepreneurial part of their makeup to be allowed to flourish.

Some founding social entrepreneurs bring friends or founding supporters onto their board; this can work well, but as the organization matures, tensions can emerge, particularly if some of the supporters have joined the staff payroll as the organization grows. The board needs to develop alongside the venture. There is a raft of experienced non-executive directors from different backgrounds who can provide sound advice, great contacts and reliable financial support.

Getting the right blend of people onto the board is crucial, as is letting the board develop. The best boards will create a great dynamic where there is a balance between adherence to detailed objectives and risk. As long as there is transparency and close identification with the vision and mission of the entity, boards will thrive.

3. Writing the right business plan

It goes without saying that every new venture must write a plan. It doesn't matter if you are a business or a charity or a social venture. There is absolutely tons of information available about how to write a business plan, and plenty of good, appropriate advice about setting up a social concern.

Of course, related to that, is how to raise the appropriate funds to sustain and run your venture. Compared with 20 years ago, there are many possible avenues. Banks have a much greater understanding about social ventures, and there are specialist organizations that can help with loans at good and reasonable rates. There is also a growing social investment sector, particularly in the UK, making funding much more readily available. You can't start without funds but, luckily, access to capital for social entrepreneurs has never been more available.

To get more general advice on starting out as a social entrepreneur, there is a lot of information available: you will need to find out what will work in your own country. For information on successful international social entrepreneurs, the Schwab Foundation,

Ashoka, the Skoll Foundation and Echoing Green will be able to give you lots of insights and inspiration, as well as potential contacts.

Conclusion

So, you have decided that you want to be a social entrepreneur. That's excellent news. The world needs you right now. Here are three final pieces of advice. First, don't worry about size. If you don't want to create a global enterprise and would rather concentrate on doing something local, then that's okay. In fact, it's much better than okay. Equally, if you think your idea could be applied internationally, then don't let anyone put you off. Second, before you start, ask an existing social entrepreneur for some advice. And third, just do it. Once you have made your decision and have everything lined up, don't pontificate. Know your own mind, don't hover at the side of the swimming pool, just jump in. It's lovely in here!

Chapter 5

Forging a more certain future for the planet

Every era has faced its own major problem. In the middle ages, it was disease. In the 19th century, it was poverty. In the first half of the 20th century, it was fascism and war on an industrial scale, while in the second half it was the looming threat of nuclear apocalypse. In the 21st century, we seem to have largely conquered all those problems and more. At least in the Western world, most of us can be fairly certain of healthy, safe and comfortable lives.

But we have another problem – one that has the potential to cause more damage than inequality, disease and war combined. We as a species are trashing the only planet that we – and millions of other species – call home. Our actions over the last 200 years – since the Industrial Revolution – have caused a huge range of problems. These include climate change, plastic and toxic pollution, topsoil erosion, water pollution and habitat destruction, to name just a few. Together, these problems represent an existential threat to humanity, indeed to the planet and all life on it. We won't go into why they are a threat – many sources will describe them more effectively than we can – but suffice to say that, unless we change our behaviour, we're in a lot of trouble.

Before we explore how we can change our behaviour and fix these problems, we need to examine the root causes of the human actions that lead to them. We are becoming more and more aware of the issues that threaten the world, and yet people – particularly governments – seem paralyzed, unable to make any meaningful change. Why?

An obsession with growth

If capitalism has a defining principle, it is that financial growth is good. You often hear leaders trumpeting a year of growth. Countries are only deemed successful if their economies continue to grow. Indeed, when an economy shrinks, it is a recession and governments implement measures to get growth back on track. But growth requires resources. We need fuel to power factories and transport, cities require space, and new products need man-made and natural materials. Those resources come from our single, finite planet. At some point, the resources will run out, and we will have plundered the Earth of all it has to give. As the economist Kenneth Boulding is credited with saying, "Anyone who believes that exponential growth can go on forever in a finite world is either a madman or an economist."

Consumerism

An economy that depends on growth depends on people spending money. Over the last century, but especially since the 1960s, advertisements have encouraged people – consumers – to buy the advertisers' products, regardless of whether they actually need them. Now, we have reached peak consumerism. Bombarded as we are by adverts – not just on television and billboards, but as we go about our day-to-day business and socializing online – we want more and more stuff. The latest phone when your old one still works fine, a new outfit to be worn once on a night out, food that gets thrown in the bin. Brands have successfully tapped into our psyches to figure out how to get us to keep buying. And while we do, landfill sites grow, and more and more resources are used. To cite a horrifying example, the Aral Sea in Central Asia, once the world's fourth largest lake, has almost entirely dried up over the last six decades thanks to the fashion industry's demand for huge amounts of water.

Globalization

In many respects, globalization is a positive force in the world. It has allowed many nations to pull themselves and their citizens out of poverty and has undoubtedly been behind the lasting peace seen in Europe. And it is only by nations working together that we can create lasting solutions to the problems that the world faces, including climate change. However, increased globalization is caused by, and causes, an increased appetite for foreign travel, both for leisure and business purposes. It has also led to an increased demand for foreign foods and products, which need to be shipped, often over great distances. The global transport sector is the fastest-growing contributor to climate emissions. In 2017, 27% of the EU's greenhouse gas emissions[2] came from the transport sector. An example of the darker side of globalization is the shipping of waste, including so-called recycling, from the Western world to developing countries. The rubbish too often ends up contaminating local soil and water systems, affecting the health of local people and local ecosystems.

Short-termism

Democracy, the opposite of dictatorship and autocracy, is largely a force for good across the world, putting power into the hands of the people. Question marks have, however, been raised around whether the model is outdated: is voting in general elections every few years for distant political figures really 'people power'? These are issues that we explore in our podcast and will investigate further in future books. The threat that democracy poses to the environment is the way it drives short-termism. Governments are normally elected for four or five years. Legislation that will have a positive effect on environmental issues, such as banning petrol-fuelled vehicles or single-use plastic, will have a painful short-term effect, making the government unpopular while they are still in power, with the benefits only being felt in the long term, when that government is long gone. It's interesting that China, although a major contributor to global carbon emissions, is taking a leading role in the fight against climate change. President Xi Jinping could be the leader for the rest of his life, so is unencumbered by elections and is able to take a more long-term view.

As we can see in the short exploration above, the problems driving environmental issues are systemic, and cannot be tackled at a simplistic, individual level. In order to ensure that the Earth and all life on it continues to thrive, all countries must put aside their differences and work together to tackle not just the issues themselves, but the causes. This is difficult but important. There is already fantastic work being done by all sorts of people, groups and governments, and we believe that the key lies in joining up their efforts and learning from those who are having the greatest impact.

Learning to live within the means of one planet

The key issue is, essentially, that we have, as a species, lost respect for the planet and are living as if we have several at our disposal. Earth Overshoot day, the date by which we have, as a planet, used up all our resources for the year, was on 29 July 2019.[3] If the whole planet lived like Americans, Earth Overshoot day would be in mid-March. Another way of looking at it is that if everyone lived like Western Europeans, we would need three planets to sustain us.

That's why social entrepreneur Sue Riddlestone co-founded Bioregional to support people, organizations and governments as they learn how to live more sustainably. In 2003, the Bioregional team created the One Planet Living framework, based on their lessons from BedZED, an eco-village they built in the UK. The framework provides ten key principles on how we can lead happy, healthy lives within the limits of the planet, leaving space for wildlife and wilderness: health and happiness; equity and local economy; culture and community; land and nature; sustainable water; travel and transport; materials and products; zero waste; zero carbon energy.[4] Developed in collaboration with the

Worldwide Fund for Nature, the framework is backed by science and experience and is highly flexible, so that people and organizations around the world can achieve a brighter, better future together.

Sue's work has extended beyond her organization. She was a driving force behind the creation and adoption of the Sustainable Development Goals – the UN's blueprint for peace and prosperity for people and the planet. She was also part of the London 2012 Olympic bid team, creating the sustainability strategy for the games, which led to the delivery of the greenest Olympic Games staged to date.

Developing the skills to be sustainable leaders

In recent times, we have seen a huge upswell in the number of individual people who want to do what they can to help the planet. There are those in the spotlight, such as Greta Thunberg and Extinction Rebellion, who create buzz and focus attention on the issues that the planet is facing. Then there are the millions of ordinary people who do what they can: cut down on single-use plastic, move toward a plant-based diet, fly less or eat locally produced, seasonal food. These are so important, as eventually we will reach a tipping point where the good outweighs the bad. However, this will take time, which we don't have. What we therefore need urgently is sustainable-thinking leaders who don't just implement planet-friendly policies, but who put the planet at the centre of their political strategies. Leaders who don't make decisions without considering the impact that those decisions will have on the planet.

Tamzin Ractliffe, a South African social entrepreneur, is focused on ensuring that as many people as possible are empowered to develop a sustainable mindset. Her Routes to Resilience initiative focuses on empowering people across society to take on the challenges that the 21st century will present – most notably the importance of living within the means of the planet. Routes to Resilience programmes seek to equip young people and professionals with the skills and competencies to identify their passion and excel in lives and livelihoods where they can lead sustainable change. They believe that resilience is a particularly important skill, allowing people to develop strategies to manage themselves and manage change. Programme participants are not just taught how to be sustainable leaders through seminars, but are given the opportunity to experience nature first-hand and also mentored through creating their own initiatives. Often from underserved communities, they finish the course confident in their power to change the world, aware of their own role in driving change, and with the 21st century skills and qualities they need to be resilient, sustainable leaders.

We are becoming more and more aware of the issues that threaten the world, and yet people – particularly governments – seem paralyzed, unable to make any meaningful change. Why?

Transforming our relationship with food

Perhaps some of these young people will go on to transform the way we eat as a planet. If so, they could do much worse than taking their inspiration from Patrick Holden and Tristram Stuart, two entrepreneurs who seek to revolutionize our approach to food and farming. Currently, the vast majority of food production globally is exploitative of the planet and livestock. Intensive arable farming degrades and depletes soil, decimates insect populations, increases susceptibility to flooding and, conversely, causes drought. Meanwhile, livestock farming uses a huge amount of water, is behind a significant proportion of deforestation and methane gas from animals, particularly cows, is a major greenhouse gas. And that's all before the food is produced: the food we throw away is a huge waste of the energy that was taken to produce it, as well as producing its own greenhouse gases as it rots.

Luckily, then, there are many social entrepreneurs working hard to find ways to fix our relationship with food and farming. Patrick Holden is a British farmer and founder of the Sustainable Food Trust, which amplifies and enhances the work of organizations that are creating farming systems that nourish the health of the planet. Regenerative agriculture – farming that is actively good for the planet, rather than simply not being bad – is possible, and the Sustainable Food Trust lobbies, campaigns and carries out research in order to spread and normalize the use of this kind of agriculture. Patrick was instrumental in the implementation of organic food standards in the UK, so transforming agriculture was a logical next step.

Tristram Stuart focuses on the other end of the farming spectrum: what happens to the food that is grown to feed us. The global food system is estimated to be responsible for around 30% of greenhouse gas emissions, but we do, of course, have to feed the world's burgeoning population. Shockingly, however, around one third of all food produced around the world is wasted[5] – that's 1.3 billion tons. All that wasted food could feed all the world's starving, undernourished people. It is wasted in a variety of ways: farmers are forced to throw away any produce that doesn't adhere to strict aesthetic standards; supermarkets dispose of any food that has passed its sell-by date; and consumers often throw away food that has passed its best-before date, even though this is often arbitrary. Tristram established his organization Feedback to advocate for a more sustainable circular food chain, one that prioritizes using surplus food to feed humans, or, if not, to feed livestock and finally, to feed soil through compost and manure. As well as pressuring governments, supermarkets and other key institutions to prioritize the issue of food waste, Feedback also runs campaigns and initiatives that help individuals rethink their food habits. These campaigns and initiatives include a network of gleaners, who work with farms to collect edible food that would otherwise be disposed of; and pressuring governments to force big business to come clean on food waste.

Tristram has also brought the issue of food waste to the beer-drinking masses. He created a recipe for beer using discarded bread; the result, Toast Ale, is sold across the UK and the US. In an unusual move, Toast Ale has made its recipe publicly available so that competitors can create and sell it too. UK supermarket Marks & Spencer is just one of many to have created a beer using Toast Ale's recipe. While seemingly a crazy move for a commercial enterprise, it makes sense when you consider that Toast Ale's main goal is not profit, but to change attitudes toward food waste.

Protecting the world's forests

The world's forests are an integral part of the wellbeing of the planet, and of so much of the life that lives on it, including humans. They directly support the lives of more than one billion people,[6] as well as the 80%[7] of terrestrial flora and fauna that call them home. A huge proportion of our food comes from fruit grown in forests, and they supply a large proportion of the drinking water for a third of the world's major cities, including New York and Mumbai. Perhaps even more fundamentally, forests are a crucial player in the future of the planet. They are one of our most powerful weapons in the fight against climate change, acting as carbon 'sinks' by absorbing carbon from the atmosphere via photosynthesis and locking it up for centuries. Humans spend billions each year on inventing technology to help us combat climate change and help us to reach our carbon emissions goals, but all over the world there are literally trillions of these natural carbon capture and storage machines, their abilities honed by natural selection over billions of years. What's more, forests also help to mitigate some of the devastating effects of climate change, including preventing flooding, reducing city temperatures, reducing pollution and keeping soil rich in nutrients.

With all this in mind, it's insane that we allow loggers, miners, farmers and many more to continue to flatten huge areas of forest. Between 1990 and 2016, the world lost 502,000 square miles (1.3 million square kilometres)[8] of forest – an area larger than South Africa. And between 30% and 60% of forests continue to be felled[9] to manufacture the products we consume.

Nicole Rycroft established Canopy to combat large-scale deforestation. Canopy works with the forest industry's largest customers and their suppliers to create solutions that protect forests. Their approach includes engaging senior business executives from industries such as publishing and fashion as champions for sustainability and conservation, empowering them to choose options that have the welfare of the forests at their heart. Canopy famously worked with the publishers of the Harry Potter series to print the books on Ancient Forest Friendly[10] paper, which is free of ancient or endangered forest fibre, made with 100% recycled or straw paper, and is whitened without chlorine.

Making fashion sustainable

Food is not alone in being an industry that needs serious transformation in order to become sustainable. Rapidly changing fashions and shortened production times are behind the rise of 'fast fashion': cheap clothing that is bought with the intention of only being worn once or twice, and then discarded. This is an environmental and social catastrophe on multiple levels. It is estimated that around 100 billion items of clothing are created each year,[11] making the fashion industry responsible for 10% of global carbon emissions.[12] This isn't even taking into consideration the huge quantity of water needed (7,600 litres for just one pair of jeans[13]), chemicals dumped into waterways and the fact that little-worn clothes, often made from nonbiodegradable fabrics, are dumped in landfill sites. The fashion industry is also an example of where environmental matters intersect with social issues: it is often women who are forced to work for very low wages to create cheap clothes, and there are even instances of child slave labour used to create clothes sold by famous Western fashion brands.

Safia Minney is a British businesswoman who pioneered a different approach to fashion. Her fashion brand, People Tree, uses organic, nonpolluting fabrics and Fair Trade-certified, transparent supply chains that ensure fair pay and the use of safe farming, dying and manufacturing processes. Critically, People Tree's products are a far cry from homespun clothes crafted from hemp that people often imagine when they think of sustainable clothing. After all, sustainability means nothing if no one will buy it.

Safia has now left People Tree to set up a consultancy to promote leadership for sustainable business and responsible supply chains. In so doing, she is propagating her expertise and experience in the subject so that more brands can put sustainability at the heart of their products, hopefully leading to a more environmentally friendly industry.

Conclusion

This chapter has only touched upon the work of a very few social entrepreneurs working to create a world that only needs one planet, and leaves room for the planet, wildlife and humans to thrive. There are hundreds, perhaps even thousands of people across the world innovating and implementing remarkable ideas to change how we relate to the planet we can currently call home. If we could harness their work and weave their principles throughout society – from big business, fashion and food to education and our everyday lives – we might have a chance of saving the world before it's too late. But we, especially those among us who lead and who have authority, need to listen to them, learn from them and be inspired to act, and quickly. We cannot rely on these remarkable people to save the world. Their work is great, and truly important, but they do not have the scale that it takes for the necessary changes to be implemented quickly.

Chapter 6

Creating more tolerant societies

Inclusion is a big topic to cover in one fairly short chapter, so we don't pretend to offer an in-depth exploration over the next few pages. Instead, we will look at the state of inclusivity in the world today and its overriding causes.

It's such a big topic because humanity is such a diverse species and, as a tribal species, we are often naturally suspicious of those who aren't like us. This means that 'diverse' often includes categories such as gender, ability, sexuality, race, class and wealth; a truly inclusive society is one that values members of each of these subgroups as much as what is perceived to be the 'norm.'

An inclusive, diverse society is a healthy one. Humans are a social species, and the effects of social isolation and loneliness on an individual are well documented, including adverse consequences for both physical and mental health. However, it affects broader society as well. Extremism, terrorism and even war are some of the most serious consequences of a society that doesn't treat all its members equally.

Inclusion and diversity go hand in hand. Diversity is the ultimate goal, while inclusion is what we must do to reach that goal. Diversity has become a much-discussed topic, with social media in particular empowering minorities to demand equality. Liberal politics, which became pervasive across much of the Western world at the end of the 20th century and beginning of the 21st is all about the rights of the individual, thus opening up the way for increased diversity and more tolerant societies.

Those conversations continue but are being increasingly challenged by the rise of populist politics. Humans are tribal, and it is inherent in us to distrust those who we believe to be different from our 'tribe,' however we define that. Populist politicians, particularly those on the right of the political spectrum, exploit that tendency for their own gain. They often appeal to people who believe their lot isn't fair and encourage them to blame their problems – whether that be a lack of jobs, money or opportunities – on the 'other.' This other will often be minority ethnic communities, regardless of how long they have lived in the country in question, who are accused of stealing jobs, taking housing and increasing crime levels. This then leads to a lack of trust, division, intolerance and racism, which itself leads to divided societies and inequality, with ethnic minorities persecuted and ghettoized. The 20th century is replete with horrific examples of where this kind of attitude can lead: the Holocaust in Nazi Germany, Apartheid in South Africa and the Rwandan genocide, to name but a few.

Populism has been on the rise in the West since the global recession of 2008. Many people lost money and livelihoods through no fault of their own and were looking for someone to blame. Populist politicians often combine populist politics ('us against the liberal elite') with anti-immigrant sentiment to appeal to those who are looking for someone to blame. It often works, as we have seen with the wave of populist leaders being elected into power or gaining prominence across the world, including US President Donald Trump, Brazil's Jair Bolsonaro, Hungarian Viktor Orban, Italy's Five Star party and the German Alternative für Deutschland (AfD).

The rise of populism seems to go hand in hand with a deterioration in the state of inclusivity across much of the West: Trump's plan to build a wall along the US's border with Mexico, anti-immigrant rhetoric in Hungary, racist attacks such as the one in a Turkish restaurant in Germany, and tightening anti-immigration policies in the UK, Australia and many other countries. Suspicion of the 'other' isn't confined to other races; Russia's gay propaganda laws have driven much of the LGBTQ+ community underground, while Jair Bolsonaro is openly homophobic.

Sometimes, a lack of diversity isn't driven by discriminatory policy, but by antipathy and a lack of action. In most of the world, women are considered equal to men in the legal sense, but in practice that is often not the case. In almost every country on the planet, women are paid less than men and are under-represented in politics and business. In too many countries, they receive fewer years of formal education than their male counterparts and are more likely to be hungry and living in poverty. They are more likely to be illiterate, die from preventable causes and be the victims of gender-based violence. Some progress is being made: Iceland, which has topped the

World Economic Forum's Gender Gap Index for 11 years, has closed almost 88% of its gender gap,[14] and other countries are implementing policies and initiatives too. However, progress is not fast enough – at the current rate of change, gender parity will only be achieved globally in 94.5 years.[15]

Homelessness is another key area that is driven by apathy and not active discrimination. A wide, complex issue that looks different in each country, it has been driven in recent years by austerity policies following the global recession of 2008 and 2009, and by increasing income inequality. In the UK, the number of homeless people in 2018 was 165% higher than in 2010, and it grew by 25% in just 12 months in London in 2018.[16]

The UK is a country with unusually high levels of income inequality compared to other developed countries. Following the global recession of 2008 and 2009, by which the UK was badly affected, funding was cut from welfare and benefits but also from health, mental health and addiction services – all of which treat some of the key drivers of homelessness. Meanwhile, the richest people in the UK continue to amass more and more money. In the two years up to 2018, the wealth of the richest 10% of households increased almost four times as fast as that of the poorest 10%.[17]

How can society address all the different types of exclusion? Each type of discrimination that falls under that umbrella term – sexism, racism, xenophobia, income inequality, homophobia, transphobia, ableism

– are so different and are large, complex issues in their own right. Addressing each will take huge, concerted efforts from governments, society and individuals across the world, with education at the heart of those efforts.

However, there could be one solution that will go a long way to forging more inclusive, tolerant societies. We all seek a sense of belonging. Creating stronger communities will go a long way to tackling discrimination as a whole, and to fostering inclusion and diversity. Communities, particularly at a micro, local level – for example, around a place of worship, sports club or village – support each other in good times and, in adversity, they rally together and take everyone along with them. They are naturally inclusive to those within the community. But perhaps even more importantly, they know each other at a human level. It is much more difficult to stereotype and be prejudiced when you understand a person's personality, what they love, what they care about and how they operate within the community.

Moreover, by dint of the fact that you are members of the same community, you have something in common: you have a common goal, whether that's the running of your village or sporting glory. That commonality is key. As the murdered British MP Jo Cox said in her maiden speech in Parliament, "We are far more united and have far more in common than that which divides us."[18]

It's important to note that, while we firmly believe that the idea of community will be integral to a successful New Ism, we should not get carried away by a fantastical idea of the community. Successful modern communities need to avoid being inward-looking and stifling – they need to open to outside influences and the opinions of others.

The economist Raghuram Rajan argues in his book *The Third Pillar* that, in order to have stability in the world, the state, markets and community need to maintain a careful equilibrium. However, he says that over the years that we've taken more power away from our cities, counties and neighbourhoods – our communities – creating a dangerous imbalance between the pillars that are responsible for many of the issues we face as a world. That has been exacerbated as organizations have become global and powerful markets, powered by the technological revolution. This globality has taken even more power away from local and regional communities.

However, strengthening communities doesn't mean just implementing policies and programmes. As César Busatto, a Brazilian Secretary of Political Coordination and Local Governance stated, "Inclusion is community … no one becomes included by being treated in a program in which they are no more than a number or statistic. Inclusion is connection to the network of community development."[19]

As always, we can look to social entrepreneurs for examples of how to create and maintain strong, cohesive, inclusive and diverse communities. Some nurture communities as a means unto itself – because communities, with the right goals, are inherently 'a good thing.' Others find that creating a community is a means to achieving other goals. Yet others find that a community is created as a happy by-product, but that the community created is a critical feature in the success of their projects.

In the latter camp is the Homeless World Cup, which uses football to inspire people who are homeless to change their own lives, but also to change attitudes about the homeless among the wider population. Their annual tournament provides a focus for, and celebration of, the work of grassroots homeless football programmes. These programmes help homeless people get themselves off the streets by giving them practical advice and support, but also a reason to want to do so – a team of fellow footballers who are relying on them. A community.

The sense of community is only heightened at the tournament, where the footballers become part of a wider community of footballers and, crucially, supporters. The tournaments attract huge crowds (168,000 in 2018 in Mexico City[20]) who see that the players are just like them – people who love sport. Being cheered on or commiserated with, rather than ignored or given handouts, allows the players to feel a sense of belonging, and that is when real change happens. If a person feels invested in a community and, critically, feels that the community is invested in them, they are more likely to find a sense of purpose and a reason to get their lives back on track. The Homeless World Cup is estimated to have changed the lives of more than 1.2 million people since 2003.[21] Eighty-three percent of the players say that their relations with their family and friends have improved since playing in the tournament, while 77% have changed their lives significantly[22] thanks to their involvement in football.

Over the last few years, millions of people have fled their homes to avoid conflict and danger, and many of them have sought refuge in the European Union (EU). The welcome from their host communities has not been as warm as they might have expected; in fact, they are often seen as a cost and a burden, which leads to social tension and division. As we have talked about earlier in this chapter, people often seek to blame societal problems on another person, and refugees are often the ideal scapegoats for a lack of jobs, high crime rates and other issues. SINGA is an organization that creates spaces where refugees, newcomers and locals can connect as equals over areas of mutual interest, such as sport, music, art and food. These groups help both the newcomers and local citizens create a sense of shared community, further integration and ultimately change perspectives. Present in France, Morocco, Germany, Italy, Belgium, Canada, Spain and the UK, it is a demonstration of the power of community to bridge divides and connect people as humans.

Hugues Benissan is a Togolese social entrepreneur who has harnessed the power of community to drive increased tolerance of homosexuality in Togo.

An inclusive, diverse society is a healthy one.

His organization, Club des 7 Jours, creates a safe environment to help the LGBTQ+ community step out of the shadows and support one another. As well as creating and nurturing this community, Club des 7 Jours identifies their needs, including healthcare and wellbeing, and trains and mobilizes members of the community itself to provide support, information and STD prevention kits to other members of the LGBTQ+ population. Club des 7 Jours has inspired the formation of other LGTBQ+ organizations, with whom they are lobbying the Togolese government to decriminalize homosexuality in the country. The power of the community is demonstrated clearly by Club des 7 Jours, with members supporting, empowering and helping one another to achieve better health and quality of life.

The remarkable organizations we have touched upon in this chapter have all created communities with a specific purpose in mind, tackling a specific problem. Comedian Sanderson Jones, however, seeks to create communities for their own sake with the knowledge that being a part of a community is an important – indeed inherent – need that humans have. Loneliness is an increasing problem in many developed countries: many who might previously have been a member of a community associated with a place of worship find themselves community-less and often very lonely. Sanderson established Sunday Assembly to address this issue. It reimagines the weekly religious congregation into a secular gathering. The format of the gatherings is familiar to anyone who has stepped foot in a place of worship: the congregation sings, listens to talks and reflects. However, the focus is very much on the creation of the community, and the benefits that it brings: connection, empathy and a shared desire to drive positive change. Sunday Assembly was established in London in the UK, but there are now over 45 'chapters' around the world.

Conclusion

In our divided world, creating diverse and inclusive societies seems like a pipe dream. The issues that drive division, exclusion and distrust of those who are different to us are very deeply rooted, and seem to get more entrenched with every year. But behind the racist, sexist, homophobic, ableist comments and the distrust between the 'haves' and the 'have nots' are human beings who are, in fact, similar. We all have people and things that we care about. If we can bring people together and ignite discussions, then perhaps we can get over the things that divide us and start to recognize the humanity in others. The other will cease to be a faceless threat but another person who is just as passionate about football, or food, or singing, as you are. It's much more difficult to hate a person than a faceless threat.

It's important to note that not all communities are a positive force, and indeed some actively aim to drive division. Even seemingly benign, village-like communities can be very conservative and stifling, unable to adapt to changing times and positive global influences. Communities need to be watchful for biases about other people. But if we can build healthy, happy communities that promote tolerance and inclusion, then perhaps we can drown out the noise from those who seek to divide us. It's a question of us all being responsible global citizens as well as local community participants.

Creating community in our age of globalization can seem difficult, but there are social entrepreneurs creating communities to overcome division. If we can learn from them and harness technology to create thriving communities around shared passions, then perhaps we can start to dismantle all the walls that have been created. The foundations of The New Ism will be its values, and a key value will be the creation of inclusive communities. How we do that, and what those communities look like, are questions that we will as a society have to grapple with, but if we can solve them, then we will be well on our way to creating a happier, more tolerant world for the next generation.

Chapter 7

Empowering young people

There is a group of people who will bear all the consequences of our actions today. They are the ones who will suffer the effects of relentless growth and climate change, of discrimination and exclusion, of the breakdown in community.

That group of people are the young. They are as diverse as humanity itself, encompassing every gender, nationality, race, religion, ability, talent, wealth bracket and sexuality. But the one thing they all have in common is that they will inherit the world that they are given by their parents and grandparents. The way we are going now, they will face the catastrophic consequences of global warming of more than the 'safe' limit of 1.5 degrees. These consequences will include more wildfires like the ones seen in Australia at the end of 2019 and the start of 2020; rising sea levels that will engulf low-lying territories, such as densely populated parts of Bangladesh and the Maldives; food scarcity as crops fail; mass wildlife extinction; and increased health problems such as respiratory issues as air quality worsens. Today's young people will also need to deal with the breakdown of communities, nationalism, discrimination and extreme inequality.

If we are to expect young people to not just face these issues that we have created, but to solve them, the very least we can do is equip them with the right knowledge and tools, and help them develop the skills they will need: resilience, creativity and problem solving. However, we are largely neglecting even these responsibilities. Education systems around the world still focus on academic disciplines that many believe are outdated and increasingly irrelevant. Meanwhile, the internet and particularly social media go unchecked, propagating bullying, mental health issues and even sexual exploitation.

Despite this, young people are increasingly finding their voices, demanding change and demanding to be heard. We see this in the climate strikes, started by teenage Swedish activist Greta Thunberg and replicated in countries across the world, with young people demanding that their leaders take urgent action against climate change. We also see it in the UK's 2017 'youthquake,' when 64% of young people voted in a snap general election[23] – up from 43% in the previous general election. In the Middle East, high unemployment and material deprivation stemming from war and the refugee crises have driven young people into the streets, demanding political and social reform. Young people were historically expected to be seen and not heard. Leadership was for older, more experienced people. It is exciting to see a generation raising their voices to demand change. The change they demand is often socially liberal and positive: these young people want to see the kind of change that improves life for many.

As ever, there are social entrepreneurs picking up where governments are unable or unwilling to establish initiatives that help young people and prepare them for the role they must take on in the future. These social entrepreneurs have found innovative ways to reach young people and educate, protect and empower them so they can achieve their potential and take the baton when the time comes.

Young people are increasingly finding their voices, demanding change and demanding to be heard.

Education

Education is correctly seen as a right, not a privilege, in much of the world. In many countries, attending school is mandatory until at least a child's mid-teens. Sadly, there are children who fall through the cracks, most notably girls in the developing world. The UN estimates that just 39% of girls living in rural areas attend secondary school, compared with 45% of rural boys, 59% of urban girls and 60% of urban boys.[24] As a result, women make up around two thirds of the world's illiterate population,[25] with a huge impact on their life and wellbeing prospects.

One social entrepreneur who has dedicated his career to tackling the issue of girls missing out on education is Saïdou Ouédraogo. He helps parents of girls in Burkina Faso understand both the causes and consequences of low school attendance in girls and works with them to develop practical solutions to the issues that prevent girls from going to school. His Mothers of Pupils Associations works with mothers (traditionally this area has been dominated by men) to learn ways to manage their daughters' education. The associations help girls attend school in other, less obvious ways as well, such as making the home environment more conducive to girls attending school and helping parents set up income-generating projects with which to pay school fees. The results of Saïdou's work are wide-ranging; not only are the daughters of parents involved in the associations more likely to go to school, but gender roles are changing. Part of the Association's work in giving girls more time to go to school is to encourage more even distribution of household chores between girls and boys as this helps change attitudes around gender roles.

One of the key purposes of education is to prepare young people for adulthood, including employment, but many feel that contemporary education is not fulfilling that goal. As the capabilities of artificial intelligence (AI) expand, robots will be able to take more and more of our jobs, which means that today's young people need to ensure they are proficient in those skills that are uniquely human, for example, creativity, problem solving, empathy, communication, teamwork and resilience.

Tom Ravenscroft is a British social entrepreneur who established Enabling Enterprise to address the chasm between education and the world of work, as well as the false perception that 'soft' skills are unmeasurable and therefore of lower priority. He developed a methodology and shared language that demonstrate that these skills are important, measurable and teachable. The Enabling Enterprise curriculum and associated online platform, which allows teachers to track the progress of their students' enterprise skills, are designed to encourage wide uptake, with the goal of this type of education eventually becoming a core part of the UK curriculum.

Sadly, even where education is mandatory for all children, children from disadvantaged backgrounds often start school with a lower level of skills and behaviours, thanks to a lack of money, resources, time or attention from their primary caregivers. The gap between advantaged and disadvantaged children often remains throughout their school careers, and that gap is a key driver of social inequality and immobility. Easy Peasy was established in the UK by Jen Lexmond to address this example of early inequality. Easy Peasy is a digital platform that brings parents together to discover, create, play and share learning games. It is constantly creating high-quality interactions for young children that nurture their development. This helps them to be at a similar developmental stage as their more privileged peers by the time they start school, setting them up for a more equal chance of success. This, of course, is a key element of social mobility – if we truly believe in equality of opportunity, we must ensure that all children start on a level pegging.

Support and protection

No matter what education they have received, children and young people are unlikely to be able to fulfil their potential if their basic needs – security, safety and love – are not met. Tragically, millions of children around the world, from the very richest countries to the very poorest, live in fear or pain, neglected by those who should care for them, whether that's their parents or the state. There are countless social entrepreneurs and charities that seek to help and support these young people, so that they can eventually go on to lead happy, fulfilled lives.

Jeroo Billimoria is an Indian social entrepreneur and one of the world's most renowned. She has founded a number of award-winning NGOs and first came to prominence for founding Childline India and Child Helpline International, kickstarting a global movement for the protection of children and youth. Childline has a simple premise: it is a telephone number that children can ring whenever they need help, support or assistance. Trained counsellors provide emergency care for children in immediate danger, but they can also be a listening ear if children need someone to talk to and link them to services that can help for their long-term care and rehabilitation. Jeroo started Childline when interacting with children staying at railway stations in Mumbai. Children in crisis would often contact her, but she realized that she couldn't respond individually to the hundreds of children who needed her help. A tele-helpline offered those children instant support when they were scared or hurt, no matter where they were. Childline or a similar service is now available in many countries across the world.

Childline identified and acted upon the fact that millions of children around the world need access to help and support and need assistance in identifying the future services that can support them longer term. Sometimes, however, those services don't work for the children in question, by virtue of the fact that they are part of an established system. Charlie Howard, a London-based psychologist, recognized that traditional therapies were incompatible with the lives of young gang members. These young people come from the most disadvantaged backgrounds and are more likely to suffer from mental illnesses such as depression, post-traumatic stress and psychosis, but are more unlikely to seek out support thanks to a distrust of authority. When they do seek support, the services are confined to specialist clinics, which might be outside their 'patch' and are too inflexible to meet the needs of this group of young people. As a result, their mental health problems are not spotted and treated until they are already in the justice system and, often, the mental health issues are a key factor in their being in the justice system in the first place.

Charlie responded to this complex situation in a seemingly simple way by taking therapy to these young people, when and where they need it. Street Therapy removes the stigma and obstacles for disadvantaged young people who need help. They self-refer and decide when they meet and for how long. They can also decide where – it could be a stairwell, a cafe, a park or while they are waiting to be seen in court. Crucially, the therapy is often delivered by people who have 'been there' as they understand what the young person is going through and their circumstances, acting as a bridge to support. As they go through therapy, they are also encouraged to join projects that help them build skills and relationships, which will help them build their lives and move into education, work or training.

Children and young people are unlikely to be able to fulfil their potential if their basic needs – security, safety and love – are not met.

Empowerment

A young person who has received a full, well-rounded education and who feels safe and supported is in a good position to tap into their potential and drive positive change themselves. Given that this generation is the one that will need to right the wrongs of their parents and grandparents, that will need to repair the damage to the planet and forge a new, more sustainable way of living for humanity, empowering them with confidence, skills and knowledge must be a priority for our current leaders. Whether they engage with politics, social entrepreneurship or simply as an active citizen doesn't matter. It's the engagement that matters, and the knowledge that they can – and must –make a difference.

Tamzin Ractliffe, who we discussed in Chapter 5, is an example of how social entrepreneurs can empower young people to engage in the most pressing issues, and step into their leadership. Her organization, Routes to Resilience, delivers programmes – often to young people from the most disadvantaged backgrounds – that imbue a sense of confidence and responsibility for the world, as well as the skills and resilience that will help them to thrive (see page 80).

Whether we like it or not, politics is the most powerful tool we have at our collective disposal to drive change. Unfortunately, young people are typically disengaged from politics. Politicians are seen variously as blinkered, untrustworthy, elitist, corrupt, out of touch and un-diverse with nothing to offer young people, so why should young people get involved? For politics to be relevant to young people, young people have to engage in politics. When a large proportion of a demographic doesn't vote, there is little incentive for politicians to create policies that appeal to those young people. In the UK general election in 2015, turnout was lowest among young people: just 43% of 18–24 year olds voted, compared to 78% of those aged 65 and over.[26] For politicians seeking higher vote share, it makes sense to create policies that appeal to older demographics more, although one would hope that chasing votes isn't their only incentive.

Michael Sani, a prominent British social entrepreneur, established his organization Bite the Ballot to address this antipathy toward politics. As a teacher at a London school, he recognized that his own apathy toward politics was reflected in his students. He set about increasing their – and his own – engagement in the political process with lunchtime clubs, which he then developed into workshops that brought politics to life. Before its closure in 2019, Bite the Ballot informed, empowered and inspired young people to embark on a journey of lifelong political engagement through a network of digital platforms. The ultimate goal was to remove barriers to youth participation in politics, thereby transforming the democratic system. Bite the Ballot's campaigns saw incredible success: they were held largely responsible for the 'youthquake' of 2017, which saw 64% of young people vote in the British general election – a 21% increase from the election two years previously.[27]

Nicola Forster has approached the issue of youth involvement in politics from a different direction. He established Foraus, a Swiss movement that brings together young people from different fields so that they can work together on the issues that matter to them. The organization has two branches: one that focuses on research and another that mobilizes and activates. The research branch produces high-quality papers for the government, which have a huge impact, while the mobilization arm organizes campaigns around elections to mobilize and inform citizens. The result of Foraus's activity is a political system that is more in tune with the needs of its young people, and a youthful population that is more engaged and can contribute to the transformation of political processes.

Conclusion

There are many social entrepreneurs and charities across the world doing crucial work to protect and support young people, ensure they receive the education they will need to thrive and empower them to become positive, active global citizens. This is so important that really it shouldn't just fall to small organizations such as the ones covered in this chapter. The work they do is groundbreaking, but they simply don't have the resources to scale, so their efforts often remain at a local or national level. Governments and other powerful institutions must prioritize young people, because if they are not educated appropriately, supported and empowered, they will not be sufficiently equipped to right the wrongs of previous generations, and then the future will look bleak indeed. Social entrepreneurs such as these offer hope and ideas for a path forward. Governments must heed their advice and take inspiration from their ideas and achievements.

Chapter 8

Restoring fairness and trust in the economic system

We live in increasingly unequal times. The current coronavirus crisis has cast even more stark light on income and wealth inequality. The poorest in society often hold the most insecure jobs, or jobs that make social distancing difficult or even impossible. At home, they often have very little space and no outside space at all, while their children's education has been interrupted as state schools don't have the resources to teach remotely, and, even if they do, access to the technology to participate in virtual lessons is restricted. Meanwhile, the wealthy and the middle classes have been able to work from home, have financial security if their jobs are at risk, have more space and have the means for their children to continue learning while not at school. Many hope that when we have come through this crisis, there will be more focus from our leaders on tackling this disparity between rich and poor.

It's important to note that the coronavirus pandemic has not increased inequality; it has just made it more obvious. In most countries across the world, inequality has risen sharply since the 1960s and 1970s, and is now at a similar level as seen in the 1920s. In 1928 and 2007 – each the year prior to major recessions – the income of the top 0.1% of US earners was more than 200 times that of the bottom 90%, while in 1975 it was just 35 times.[28] This trend is echoed in China, India, Russia and more moderately in Europe.

Most of us are familiar with the shocking statistics around share of wealth. For example, the richest 1% of people own 45% of global wealth,[29] while the richest ten men in the world have a greater combined wealth than most individual countries in the world, including wealthy ones such as Saudi Arabia and Switzerland.[30]

Income inequality is also a driving force behind the rise of extremist politics, social unrest, higher crime levels and lower average education attainment. It also goes hand in hand with poor health. A country's average life expectancy and obesity and child mortality rates are all linked to the inequality in its population.[31] The US, for example, is the wealthiest country in the world, but, alongside China, it also has the highest inequality of the world's wealthiest nations.[32] Its average life expectancy is four years lower than that of most other equitable countries, while its infant mortality rate is 5.7 deaths per 1,000 live births. In Iceland, which has far lower income inequality, that number is just 1.6.[33]

There are many drivers of income inequality; indeed, some inequality is inevitable in a capitalist, market-driven system. But our current trading and financial systems only serve to perpetuate the problem when in fact they could, as demonstrated by some of the world's leading social entrepreneurs, become part of the solution.

Trade

Trade is a term with a very broad definition: the sale and purchase of goods and services. It covers all transactions where a customer pays for something and is at the very heart of our modern capitalist system. For the purposes of this chapter, we will focus on trade as the exchange of goods such as food or clothing for money.

Many of the goods we purchase in the Western world reach our shops via long and complex supply chains, with each player or 'middleman' taking their slice of the profit at each stage. That means that the original producers and workers, at the very bottom or start of the chain, receive very little of the profit from that product, particularly if they are in the developing world. This is only exacerbated by the fact that, in the West, we have come to expect that goods should be cheap – but someone has to pay. That is how we have ended up with the notorious sweatshops, where workers are forced to work in extremely poor conditions for long hours and for very low wages. Rana Plaza, the clothing factory where many clothes destined for Western fashion stores were made by workers living below the poverty line, collapsed in 2013, killing 1,134 people.

Our obsession with cheap is also why we have so many farmers of products like coffee and cocoa living in abject poverty, even though they work their land and themselves as hard as they can. The way things currently work, it's a race to the bottom. How much more can we take advantage of vulnerable people, ignoring their plight just because they are so far away, and we want cheap stuff?

The Fair Trade movement was established to address these issues. It puts people and the planet first by promoting better prices, decent working conditions, environmental sustainability and Fair Trade terms for farmers and workers in the developing world. By requiring participating companies to pay fair, sustainable prices that are always at or above the market rate, the movement empowers the people who make our food and the goods we buy to lift themselves out of poverty and take control of their own lives. The impact is fourfold: ensuring income sustainability for some of the world's poorest people, empowering them to make the best decisions for themselves, their families and their communities, promoting individual and community wellbeing, and environmental stewardship.

The Fair Trade movement exists in different forms internationally. One of its pioneers is Paul Rice, a social entrepreneur who founded Fair Trade USA. We interviewed him for our podcast in 2018, in which he explained that his vision is that 'fair' trade just becomes normal. People who grow food for others to eat, and who make the clothes we wear, should be able to afford to feed and clothe themselves and their families.

Safia Minney, who we mentioned in Chapter 5, is another social entrepreneur who has helped to transform trade back to what it should be – beneficial for all parties. The fashion industry is notorious for its terrible record in both how workers are treated and the impact that it has on the environment, particularly with society's increasing hunger for so-called 'fast fashion' – cheap, often poorly made clothes that are only intended to be worn a few times before being thrown away. The brand that Safia established, People Tree, prioritizes the highest ethical and environmental standards as well as style and was the first Fair Trade fashion company.

Businesses like People Tree that sell Fair Trade products don't just ensure that the producers they work with are fairly paid and fairly treated; they also allow consumers to vote with their wallets, demonstrating that they want supply chains that are fair and sustainable. As Safia told us on The New Ism podcast, we must value the Earth's resources and the people who make our clothes and other products: buying fairly traded goods is a way that we can do this.

Finance

The way in which global financial systems are set up in the capitalist model is incredibly complex: very few people fully understand where money comes from, how it moves within and between markets, and how it is used by governments and institutions. That lack of understanding leads to a lack of trust, both in money itself and in the institutions that control it. It's very difficult to trust something you don't understand. Trust was further broken down following the financial crash of 2008–2009. As most people saw it, the banks were responsible for the crash and its dire consequences, which reverberated through societies around the world, but were nonetheless bailed out by governments who considered the banks 'too big to fail.' Interestingly, in the current coronavirus crisis, many governments have had to come up with a huge amount of money to fight the virus and attempt to shore up their respective economies, which has left many wondering where this money was during the crisis of 2008–2009 and beyond.

Another basic flaw of our current financial system is that it is set up to favour those who already have money. A rich person who has invested their money with the help of an expert can essentially live off the interest that their investments drive, without needing to work, while billions around the world strive to earn just enough to live off. Many can't even do that. This dichotomy throttles the very entrepreneurialism that capitalism is meant to promote.

The very poorest and most disadvantaged people in the world are all too often unable to access even tiny loans from established lenders, as their needs are not profitable for the lenders, and banks are reluctant to lend to people with little or no credit history. Without these loans, it's very difficult to establish the small businesses that could help lift them and their families out of poverty, and so the poverty cycle continues. Muhammad Yunus, perhaps one of the world's most famous social entrepreneurs, created the concept of the microloan in order to help break this cycle and give poor people a hand up, rather than the more traditional handout. Yunus reversed conventional ideas of how banking worked by removing the need for collateral or a credit rating. The bank that he established in 1983, Grameen Bank, makes microloans to some of the poorest people in Bangladesh and India. The bank's model is based on the concept that a person is more likely to repay their loan if they are 'peer pressured' into doing so. Each borrower must belong to a five-person group, who all ensure that the loan is repaid, and borrowers are encouraged to save money so that they can always make repayments.

Women, particularly very poor women, have historically found it much more difficult than men to secure loans, meaning that it is even more difficult for them to lift themselves out of poverty, leaving them more dependent on men. Grameen Bank identified that women are, in fact, very reliable borrowers and astute entrepreneurs. Indeed, it is a generally recognized fact that one of the best ways to help a community is to support its women, as they are more likely to spend their money on their families and their households than men are. Ninety-seven per cent of Grameen's borrowers, known as members, are women.[34] The loans they have taken out have empowered them to raise their status within their communities, reduce the dependency they have on their husbands and improve the diets and living standards of their children.

Grameen Bank's results are quite remarkable: it is estimated that the average household income of Grameen Bank members is around 50% higher than that of a similar household in a village not covered by the bank. The bank claims that only 20% of its members live below the poverty line, compared to 56% of comparable non-Grameen bank members.[35] In 2006, Muhummad Yunus and Grameen Bank won the Nobel Peace Prize.

It's not just in poorer countries where the poor have limited access to credit. People living in low-income, marginalized communities even in wealthy, developed countries such as the UK also have limited access to high-quality financial products and services, despite the fact that they are most in need of them. This makes them vulnerable to loan sharks and 'payday lenders,' who charge extremely high interest and who were, until relatively recently, largely unregulated in the UK. Reliance on these types of lenders regularly led to crippling debt for those who could least afford it, and the stress related to that kind of debt can lead to issues such as depression, substance misuse, other health issues and even suicide.

Faisel Rahman is a British social entrepreneur who, early on in his career, worked for Grameen Bank. While he was there, Muhammad Yunus explained to him that there are people who need money and they are good risks; just because you don't know that, doesn't mean they're a bad risk. It's your job to figure that out. That was the inspiration behind Fair Finance, which Faisel founded to transform the provision of high-quality products and services for those who most need them but often cannot access them because of a poor credit rating or not having one at all. Fair Finance offers a range of high-quality financial products and services, including loans and advice, which are both affordable and accessible. They also show the mainstream financial sector, including retail banks, that providing services to the most marginalized people can be both safe and profitable, as long as the correct information is provided.

Faisel was one of the first guests to appear on The New Ism podcast. During our conversation, he explained to us that the financial system was built on trust with the word 'credit' coming from the Latin 'credo,' meaning to believe or trust. The pieces of the financial system, from the smallest to the largest, are built on the relationship between two people, and Faisel himself found that from the very beginning of Fair Finance, he was making decisions on whether to lend based on whether he trusted the person in front of him. The mainstream financial system has forgotten this trust, now making their decisions according to algorithms or spreadsheets.

But that's not all. Faisel says that the fundamental difference between Fair Finance and the mainstream system is the 'flow' of trust. It's not just the trust that the lender has in the borrower that is important. Most people who have been mistreated by the mainstream financial system of course don't trust the system, so they don't borrow. Faisel works on the basis that if you want to change the paradigm of people not borrowing and not paying their debts, you have to convince them that you are trustworthy, that you are worth paying.

Women, particularly very poor women, have historically found it much more difficult than men to secure loans, meaning that it is even more difficult for them to lift themselves out of poverty, leaving them more dependent on men.

Taxes

Trust – or a lack thereof – also lies at the heart of another fundamental financial mechanism. Taxes. Hugely controversial and at the heart of many a political manifesto, taxes are what citizens and organizations pay governments to carry out public services, whether that's healthcare, welfare or infrastructure. To put it another way, people hand over their money to governments and trust that they will carry out the role of 'social protector,' doing what needs to be done to ensure the health, safety and comfort of the country. However, in so many countries around the world, that trust has broken down. People do not trust their leaders and therefore resent paying taxes, and there are plenty of people around the world who go to great lengths to avoid paying their taxes. It is interesting to note that in the Nordic countries, where they pay some of the highest taxes in the world, trust in governments and one another is among the highest in the world (in fact, trust has been referred to as the Nordic 'gold').

Taxes are also a way to redistribute wealth. As we discussed earlier in this chapter, income and wealth inequality is becoming more and more stark, with wealth being concentrated within a smaller and smaller number of families. This results in extremes of wealth and poverty, which in turn causes animosity and social tension. This disparity could be corrected with tax policies that still allow people to be wealthy and have more than others, but also ensure that people on the other end of the spectrum have the basic services they need to live healthy, fulfilled lives. To take the Nordic example again: these countries pay some of the highest taxes and have the lowest inequality scores in the world; the fact that they also have high levels of social trust cannot be unrelated.

Taxes have been with us almost since the beginning of time, and it is inherent to our economic system. It is difficult to imagine a world without taxes. How would we pay for public services? Would citizens have to pay charities or private enterprises to collect waste, run hospitals, build sewers and maintain roads?

The balance between governments paying for public services and charities or philanthropists stepping in is an interesting one. In the US, for example, taxes are low compared to other developed countries, but there are around 1.5 million not-for-profit organizations[36] and many philanthropists who provide many of the services that you might expect from a government. At the other end of the spectrum, Chinese people pay high taxes, but the state takes care of everything and, as such, there are fewer charities in China than in the US. Which system is better? There are positives and negatives for both.

We believe that a new, fairer economic system will be based on taxes, but those taxes will need to be raised in a transparent way, and people need to understand and trust how their money will be used. They need to see a correlation between the taxes they pay and the benefits they see, both for themselves and for society, and then they will be happy to pay.

Conclusion

In order to transform the global financial and trading systems, we must base them around trust. Trust is fundamental to the work of all the social entrepreneurs that we have looked at in this chapter and throughout this book. Trust will be a key value at the heart of any fair, inclusive system, and it has to imbue societies, from the community level right up to leadership and between nations. It is a concept that seems to have been disappearing over the last few decades, so how can we start to build it up again?

One thing is certain: trust cannot exist where there is not peace, and a breakdown in trust is always at the heart of tensions, which can overspill into violence and war. Trust and peace need one another.

Chapter 9

Creating peaceful societies

When we think of peace, we tend to think of it as the opposite of war. If a country is not at war with itself or with another state, it is peaceful. This absence of war is, of course, a hugely important indicator of peace: war was, until relatively recently, the biggest killer of human beings. However, peace is more than just the absence of war: it is also the opposite of violence, extremism, community division and disagreement.

War

While news headlines may suggest differently, we are currently living through one of the most peaceful times in human history.[37] Of course, there are many devastating wars ongoing at the time of writing, including in Syria, Yemen and Libya, but much of the world is at peace, both internally and with other nations. The contributing factors to this seemingly lasting peace are complex and varied. They include increased globalization and international trade, the existence of international bodies such as the EU, NATO and the United Nations and, less positively perhaps, mutually assured destruction. The period of relative peace in Europe since the end of the Second World War – Pax Europaea – was largely thanks to increased cooperation between countries that were on opposing sides in the world wars. The EU was awarded the Nobel Peace Prize in 2012.

Despite this lasting peace, the majority of countries remain poised for war. According to the CIA, only 36 countries worldwide[38] *do not* have an army, and many of the richest states invest billions of dollars each year in weaponry and war preparations. Nine countries

– the US, China, Russia, France, the UK, India, Pakistan, North Korea and Israel – have nuclear weapons or are understood to have them.

The arguments for and against such huge spending and the possession of such destructive capabilities rage, but they have taken on even greater pertinence of late. In this era of stability and peace, our greatest enemy is not other nations, but pathogens. This book is being written in lockdown as coronavirus sweeps across the world, claiming more than 400,000 lives so far[39] – that is not far off the number estimated to have been killed in Syria's brutal civil war.[40] That leads many to raise the question of why are we not spending more on health defence, money that could feasibly be taken from military spending, given that our armies and weapons are so rarely at war? The US spends $649 billion a year on defence.[41] Would more lives have been saved if that had been invested into a universal national health service? More than 100,000 people have died of coronavirus in the US.[42]

One social entrepreneur who works to drive lasting peace is Helena Puig Larrauri, a Spaniard whose organization, Build Up, identifies and empowers a wide range of grassroots peace-building individuals and organizations to participate more deeply in peace processes. These grassroots players include victims of conflict – especially women and children – and local communities that are normally given a voice in high-level negotiations. The approach ensures that peace processes are more representative, as well as empowering communities to take greater ownership. This makes it much more likely that the peace will be enduring, as people at a local level have contributed to its creation so are invested in making it last. Build Up's methodology has been implemented in peace processes across the world, including in Colombia, South Sudan and Somalia.

James Wuye and Mohammed Ashafa are a Christian pastor and Muslim cleric, respectively, who work together to prevent conflict between Christians and Muslims in Nigeria. These conflicts cost thousands of lives and do untold damage to individuals and communities, which further embeds religious hatred. Pastor Wuye and Imam Ashafa believe that the only way to reduce these clashes is by having leaders of each faith promote religious teachings of peace and nonviolence, and support one another in dampening tensions. An example of when this worked was in the wake of the publication of highly controversial cartoons featuring the Prophet Muhammad in the Netherlands. They stoked religious tension globally, including in Nigeria. In response, James and Mohammed asked Christian leaders to publicly condemn the cartoons, and Chief Imams to accept the condemnation and encourage calm. The approach was successful. This simple but highly effective strategy has been expanded upon, with James and Mohammed creating programmes for schools to promote peace and understanding.

In this era of stability and peace, our greatest enemy is not other nations, but pathogens.

Extremism

One of the blights of the modern world is extremism. Extremists hold an extreme ideology or belief. In the UK, extremism is defined as the vocal or active opposition to the UK's fundamental values, including democracy, the rule of law, individual liberty, and respect and tolerance for different faiths and beliefs.[43] As this definition (which is similar in nations across the world) suggests, extremism is diverse and rooted in many ideologies, including religious, political and racial. Extremism is the most frequent driver of terrorist acts, which kill thousands each year: more than 32,000 globally in 2018 alone.[44]

The causes of extremist thinking and behaviour are far too extensive and complex to explore properly in these pages, but one of the myriad causes of this antithesis of peace is war itself, particularly what is seen by many as the propensity of Western states to get involved in foreign, often domestic conflicts. It is also caused by isolation from society. Many Islamic extremists, for example, are citizens of Western nations who feel disenchanted by, and separate from, Western society and are seduced by the messages of radical preachers.

Islamic extremism is often the form of radicalization that comes to mind first, particularly in the West. However, other forms of extremism are equally toxic and destructive. White supremacism, far-right extremism (the latter and former are often linked), left-wing extremism and single-issue extremism, such as some (but by no means all) animal rights and anti-LGBTQ+ movements. Each of these need to be understood and addressed before we can claim to have truly peaceful societies.

The flames of ideological extremism are often fanned in the prison system, so that a young person with nascent extremist tendencies can emerge months or years later as a fully-fledged extremist, ready to commit violent acts for their beliefs. Judy Korn, a German social entrepreneur, has created a rehabilitation programme that helps young offenders interrupt and break the vicious cycle of frustration, fanaticism, violence and reoffending. Judy's organization, Violence Prevention Network, addresses the complex roots of the young person's offences – for example ideological, social and behavioural – helping them become more resilient to extremist influences both while in prison and when they have been released, and more likely to abstain from acts of violence. Judy's methodology, which works on the basis that young people must be given a second chance, proved highly effective for this difficult group, and has been expanded to encompass all violent young offenders.

Violence at a community and family level

Even the country – sadly, only theoretical for now – that refrains from warmongering and has no extremism in its society, cannot claim to be peaceful. Every society, from the very richest to the very poorest, suffers from extreme violence at a community and family level. As ever, there are a myriad of causes. Domestic violence is a huge problem globally, particularly for women and children. One of the many terrible consequences of the coronavirus pandemic is that, with many families stuck at home, domestic violence is on the increase and victims have nowhere to turn.

Gender violence is tragically common across the world, with a third of women experiencing physical or sexual abuse.[45] In Latin America, with its traditional patriarchal culture, the problem is particularly severe: 14 of the countries with the highest rates of femicide by a partner are in the region.[46] Daniela Maudeth Valdivia Gutiérrez is a Bolivian social entrepreneur who is seeking to put an end to gender-based violence in Bolivia. She leads a movement that shifts the narrative around how women should be treated and what masculinity looks like. Critically, men play a key role in the movement.

Daniela's organization, Huellas & Futuro (Footprints & The Future), works with schools so that children grow up viewing men and women as equals, but also institutions such as military academies and the police, which unintentionally promote out-of-date narratives on gender roles that could justify violence toward women. Daniela also runs media campaigns to raise public awareness of the issue.

Gang-related violence is also an issue faced by most countries. It looks different nation by nation: whether it's the activity of the mafia in southern Italy, the terrible violence and terror meted out by Mexico's drug cartels, or the stabbings of young Londoners by other young people in rival gangs. However, there are often similarities: the worst violence is seen in deprived urban areas, and illegal drugs are frequently a factor, whether it's the large-scale movement of drugs to the US from Mexico, or drug dealing in the UK's county lines.

Young people often join gangs to achieve a sense of belonging. They frequently have chaotic home lives and gangs offer a sense of community and stability that they can't get elsewhere. This is true around the world, from the UK to El Salvador. In Thailand, Laddawan Chaininpun watched in horror as her 12-year-old grandson joined a notorious gang in Chiang Mai, but she knew that no amount of threatening or pleading would dissuade him. While he came from a loving family, the gang offered him what he needed at that stage in his life. After spending years working to understand young people in gangs, Laddawan established the Chiangmai Youth Community Centre (CYC), which enlists gang members as part of the solution to the problem of gang violence. The key to her approach was working with gangs to strengthen the bonds between them, based on her understanding that the gangs offer a much-needed support network to members. Laddawan brought rival groups together to solve conflicts and establish rapport, and created partnerships with institutions and individuals such as the police, parents and social workers to break down the stigma associated with gang membership, which often only serves to exacerbate antagonism toward society and violence. Ultimately, Laddawan and CYC helps young people see their own value and understand that they can contribute positively toward society.

Division and intolerance

A lack of peace doesn't always mean physical harm and death. It can result from divisive politics and public discourse. Two notable and perhaps obvious examples are Trump's America and Brexit Britain. Humans have a desire to belong, to be part of a tribe. One of a national leader's key roles should be to unite, as far as possible, a population behind a common purpose, thereby lessening division. Unfortunately, the tendency toward populism we are seeing in many countries at the moment is leading to increased division and intolerance, as we explored in Chapter 6. Leaders such as Donald Trump and Jair Bolsonaro embody the 'divide-and-conquer' route to power, highlighting and exacerbating fault lines through the societies of their respective countries. The UK's decision to leave the EU was similarly tribal, summed up by the distinction between the 'somewheres' (often socially conservative people who live in small towns and villages) and the 'anywheres' (socially liberal, university-educated and living in cities).

Tensions and division such as these are unpleasant but bearable, particularly when compared to the plight of people caught in the crossfire between differing opinions in places such as Syria. And that is where the issue lies. Simmering tensions can sometimes boil over into violence and even war, which is why it's so important to create more harmonious societies.

Ruth Ibegbuna is a British social entrepreneur who, in the wake of the UK's decision to leave the EU, was disturbed by the divisive and hate-filled rhetoric that sprang up as a result of the referendum campaign and only worsened as the country tried to work out how best to deliver on the result of the vote. The country quickly divided into two tribes – 'Remainers' and 'Leavers' – who filled the media and social media with judgments about the other side. Ruth established the Roots Programme as a way to overcome these divisions, based on the idea that society benefits if people can find ways to identify with people who are different to them. The programme identifies people from very different communities – working class community leaders and senior figures in business and politics, or bright students at state and private schools – and brings them together to eat, talk and debate the issues that affect everyone, no matter their background. As we discussed in Chapter 6, it's much more difficult to hate someone if you know and understand them personally, particularly when you find that you agree on some issues.

French social entrepreneur Stéphane de Freitas has the same ambitions. His organization, Eloquentia, equips young people, particularly from disadvantaged areas, with the skills and support they need to be able to articulate their experiences and frustrations, thereby increasing dialogue between different sections of society. He has also established Indigo, an international nonprofit social network that aims to reconfigure the social bond and revolutionize access to goods and services with a 'digital tool of solidarity' based on a virtual generosity-based currency, the Digo.

Conclusion

We've discussed peace as a mainly domestic issue in this chapter, but of course many of the most bitter wars are fought between countries, with the two world wars in the first half of the 20th century being the most obvious examples. Even between countries ostensibly at peace, there is often toxic rhetoric based on blaming 'the other' for the ills experienced by citizens. By extension, national boundaries – those most artificial of boundaries – are the creators of tension and even war. In our increasingly connected and globalized times, and in a world where the most serious problems, including climate change, are global problems, we need to be able to put aside prejudices and blame, and work together to tackle these global issues. We are all human after all.

This question of nationalism versus globalism, the desire to be from somewhere in a world that is so seamlessly connected, comes up a lot in The New Ism podcast. We enjoy the perks of being global citizens – holidays in far-flung places, exotic foods on our supermarket shelves, cheap clothing – but we simultaneously want our national identity. That can be a good thing, as pride in one's roots and a feeling of belonging is a very human desire. But it can also be negative, for example, when patriotism becomes nationalism, and when nationalism turns into xenophobia and racism.

We must ask ourselves: does our insistence on a national identity contradict our desire to be global citizens? Does the notion of the nation have a role in a New Ism, or should we rethink our sense of belonging? Can we be citizens of the world and simultaneously a citizen of a country? We don't yet have the answer to these questions, but we are exploring them, and the answer will become a central value of a New Ism.

Chapter 10

Forwards towards a New Ism

Throughout this book we have highlighted the inspirational work carried out by exceptional social entrepreneurs.

You might not have heard of most of them. This is because they tend to be humble people, and they are consumed with their work at the coalface. Some are very focused on their own area and are determined to make a big difference in one particular community. Others have gone to scale and have rolled out their organizations around the globe. Some have even created concepts like microfinance or Fair Trade, which have been picked up and replicated by others.

They are applauded when they speak. Some have been given high-ranking awards for their efforts. Many have been recognized and have become fellows of global networks that promote social entrepreneurship and, crucially, their combined impact is massive. They are making a huge difference to people's lives and the environment.

According to the Schwab Foundation for Social Entrepreneurship Impact Report, published in January 2020, 622 million people's lives have been improved as a result of the efforts of social entrepreneurs in the past 20 years.[47] And that's only from the social entrepreneurs in that particular network. The combined effort for all social entrepreneurs around the world is massive. That effort is rightly acclaimed and applauded.

Critics will ask, "So what?" They would argue that, while the work and impact of the social entrepreneurs is indeed to be applauded, they shouldn't have to exist in the first place. But is that right? Are we saying that social and environmental issues are solely the fiefdom of government? Surely we need people to stand up about some of the more challenging issues of the day and take practical action in a constructive way?

Change is taking place at a breath-taking pace and governments can be slow to react. Meanwhile, social entrepreneurs have it within their very DNA to be nimble, smart and effective. But as the sector for social entrepreneurship becomes more defined, where do social entrepreneurs fit into society's ecosystem?

Traditionally, society can be split into three sectors: public, private and voluntary. Social entrepreneurs are put into the voluntary basket, but this doesn't accurately describe what they do. A better way to classify them might be as sitting between the voluntary and business sectors, combining the characteristics of both. Many social entrepreneurs will say they have adopted business models in order to create social and environmental impact. But many also connect with governments and collaborate to create changes in policy. Another way of looking at social entrepreneurs is to see them as being a newly emerging sector that touches all sides of the traditional sectors but stands separately.

This creates further questions. Shouldn't governments and other parts of society be doing the work that social entrepreneurs do? Where there are societal challenges, social entrepreneurs can come up with solutions, given their inherent ability to innovate, but governments should step in and scale their solutions.

One claim we heard early in the emergence of this sector was: "Social entrepreneurs will appear and thrive where there is 'social market' failure." That seems to be a sensible statement. You find many more social entrepreneurs in Bangladesh compared with Scandinavia, for example.

This does not mean that the clichéd view of the West knowing best and being obliged to help poorer developing countries prevails. There are many social entrepreneurs in the US, the richest country in the world with an economy roughly 80 times the size of Bangladesh's. Social market failure can occur in any country regardless of its economic performance and level of wealth. It can occur anywhere.

That is when we start exploring the idea of whose responsibility it is to address social market failure. Let's take two examples: extreme poverty and climate change.

First, poverty. There shouldn't be any extreme poverty in a world with so much wealth. No one we know disagrees with that statement, but who is taking responsibility to end extreme poverty? Statistics show that global poverty levels have dropped considerably over the past two decades. One of the big reasons for that fall has been the economic transformation in China, which has lifted millions out of poverty. The fall in poverty is the result of economic policies and planning pursued by the Chinese government, rather than charities or social entrepreneurs, of which there are very few.

However, there have also been big decreases in poverty levels in Africa and South America, where charities and social entrepreneurs have been working hard for the past two decades. While there are still many problems associated with poverty in the world, exacerbated by a global economic system that is increasing the gap between the wealthiest people and the poorest, we should be clear that many interventions have been successful and should be recognized.

It's not all doom and gloom, but the challenge is that the success is not systemic. This is where the debate needs to move on to next. It's why we are creating the debate around a New Ism, because although there is plenty of great work going on, there is no real fundamental change taking place in the systems that can create poverty.

We seem to accept as a society that we will always have food banks, because there will always be people who cannot afford to buy food for themselves and their families. Many people are kind enough to give food to food banks; indeed, this is the type of practical concept that social entrepreneurs often come up with when the need emerges. Food banks are simple and effective, and have a positive impact on the lives of thousands, if not millions, of people. However, there shouldn't be a need for food banks in the first place, because it should be a given that everyone is able to feed themselves. We shouldn't allow food banks to become an accepted part of everyday life.

The same goes for homelessness, which is rife in almost every country in the world. We have come to accept that there are people who sleep on the streets. There are many effective, impactful interventions that help homeless people rebuild their lives and re-enter society. The challenge is that as soon as one homeless person moves on, another takes their place. If we truly want to create a society where nobody is homeless – and many believe that is possible – then you need systemic change.

Turning away from the example of poverty, we move onto a second example of social market failure: the environment, or, rather, the failure of humanity to look after the planet. Huge numbers of people around the world are concerned about climate change and how we are potentially destroying our planet. Once again, social entrepreneurs are at the forefront of the response, creating all manner of sustainable entities that are preserving our environment in practical ways.

Some of these initiatives are tiny and some citizens, particularly young people, are changing their lifestyles so that they cause less damage to the environment. These are miniscule actions when taken in isolation, but, if everyone followed suit, then the impact would be massive. Movements are growing as we begin to understand the negative consequences of our lifestyles. People have finally woken up to the damage being caused by plastic, for example, and are taking action accordingly, but so much more needs to be done.

The central challenge for the current economic system is how to stop our obsession with growth when growth is the central driver for our economy, and, indeed, how we measure success. The planet is finite. Therefore, we cannot keep growing infinitely. That is just common sense. We have to create an economic system that is not based solely on economic growth.

Green activists will argue that we should buy fewer clothes, and that those we do buy should be recycled or swapped when we no longer want them. Of course, this makes sense, but what happens to the people employed by the fashion industry, many of whom are some of the poorest people in the world? We need to create a new economic model that has sustainability, not growth at its core, and works out ways to thrive even as it contracts. The challenge is, how do we create a thriving clothing sector when it produces less?

Some businesses are beginning to wake up to this challenge. A number are of the opinion that it is better to work in a good world rather than a bad world, and that the business sector has major obligations to the community around it. It must put something back. Although some businesses are adopting genuinely beneficial corporate social responsibility (CSR) policies, many more are accused of simply 'greenwashing' and obsessing about the bottom line and shareholder return at the expense of everything else, including the planet.

You can see the potential of the emergence of a coherent social entrepreneurial sector that can connect with governments that want to adopt policies fit for the modern world, but which are bound by archaic systems. A thriving social entrepreneurial sector can also connect with businesses that genuinely understand the role they have to play in a world where growth for growth's sake is no longer feasible.

If that sector is to emerge and thrive, then it requires some careful thinking. It needs a clear set of values with which all players can connect. At the moment, many social entrepreneurs are stuck on the coalface doing heroic work with inadequate resources and are consequently disconnected with their fellow social entrepreneurs. They are dealing with the social and environmental failure of society as best they can and have little opportunity to look outward.

Perhaps the situation could be described in another way. Many social entrepreneurs are sticking their fingers in the holes of a leaking dam and are praised for keeping the water at bay, but no one is looking at the dam in its entirety. Either we will end up with lots of social entrepreneurs heroically holding up the dam and being worn out in the process, or the dam will come crashing down despite their best efforts. Wouldn't it be better to think about how we can create a stronger, leak-proof dam?

The advance of technology has been startling over the past two decades, and all of us have been impacted by it in one way or another. While some of these advances have greatly improved our lives, we seem to be more individually and collectively stressed than ever before. Technology allows things to happen at a greater speed than ever before, and that places huge strain on human beings. Part of this strain comes from how society is currently being melded together.

In the UK, for example, the Church used to take on most of the responsibility for looking after the poorest in society. After the end of the Second World War in 1945 and with the birth of the welfare state, the responsibility shifted to the government. However, as successive administrations have moved toward a philosophical belief in smaller government and the public votes for political parties that promote lower taxes, the government has tried to retreat from its role as a welfare provider. Into that void have stepped charities and social enterprises that have been able to eke out funding through donations from the public. In one sense, it could be called a 'voluntary tax,' but that means that charities are only as effective as the generosity of the public allows them to be. Some argue that the charity or voluntary sector is overcrowded and grossly inefficient, so the level of care and support for a population that is increasingly stressed is patchy or simply absent.

What we need is some coherent thinking. If, for example, the public sector is backing out of its role as a welfare provider and is incapable of developing effective environmental planning for the future, then who will take on that responsibility? Clearly, there is a huge opportunity for social entrepreneurs to provide a clear vision on what that space might look like, and even to provide effective leadership that creates sustainable impact.

But, to do that, we need to agree that that is what is happening. There needs to be a very clear shift that changes how the roles of the public, private and voluntary sectors are defined, if indeed those sectors are still relevant. But there also needs to be a shift in political thinking so that it becomes and remains relevant to the modern world.

Much economic thinking is defined by the left and the right of the political spectrum and where an individual places themselves on that spectrum. To take the example of the role of government, people are said to be on the right if they favour 'smaller' government with greater involvement of the private sector, while people on the left prefer the opposite. Social entrepreneurs are normally classified as being on the left, as they are often highly critical of current systems and work with people who are excluded and vulnerable. However, almost none of the social entrepreneurs we have met through our podcast and, indeed, throughout our careers would put themselves on the left or the right. They see themselves as working in a different orbit altogether, completely separate from the traditional left-versus-right political debate. They want to create a new system in which neither left nor right (nor the middle for that matter) are correct or even relevant.

However, it's not clear what that system looks like. Intuitively, social entrepreneurs know that the current system doesn't work and that the traditional left-versus-right arguments are contained within the media, which is obsessed with labelling. They also know that they are in the process of creating something new that is much more positive, but which hasn't yet been defined. They know they are part of something bigger, but they will admit to not being able to articulate exactly what it is.

The foundation of any new system needs to be clear about the values upon which it is based. When those values have been identified, it is a question of freeing the mind of old adages and truisms such as left versus right, creating new concepts that encapsulate those values and forging new, practical policies that reflect the work that social entrepreneurs are doing on a daily basis right now.

It will be challenging, and it is why we are creating this series of books about what we are calling The New Ism. We desperately need a new system that is based on fairness, community and sustainability. It can be created by, or inspired by, social entrepreneurs, but there are many challenging issues that need to be thought through and articulated before a new coherent system that people can believe in starts to emerge.

The journey begins here. We need to hear *your* views and *your* voice. Be practical, be constructive and be creative. We invite you to listen to our podcasts, where we interview many of the social entrepreneurs mentioned in this book, read our blogs and become a supporter of our bid to create a fairer, more sustainable future.

Over to you.

www.newismtalks.com

Many social entrepreneurs are sticking their fingers in the holes of a leaking dam and are praised for keeping the water at bay, but no one is looking at the dam in its entirety.

Endnotes

CHAPTER 1

1. 'Local Elections in England, May 2018,' The Electoral Commission, August 2018, https://www.electoralcommission.org.uk/sites/default/files/pdf_file/May-2018-Electoral-Data-Local-Elections-Report.pdf

CHAPTER 5

2. 'Greenhouse gas emissions from transport in Europe,' European Environment Agency, December 17 2019, https://www.eea.europa.eu/data-and-maps/indicators/transport-emissions-of-greenhouse-gases
3. 'Earth Overshoot day: living beyond our means,' Deutsche Welle, August 8 2016, https://www.dw.com/en/earth-overshoot-day-living-beyond-our-means/a-19444507
4. 'One Planet Living: making it easier to live happily and sustainably,' Bioregional, Last accessed April 17 2020, https://www.bioregional.com/one-planet-living
5. 'Food wastage footprint: Impacts on natural resources – summary report,' Food and Agriculture Organization of the United Nations (FAO), September 2013, http://www.fao.org/3/i3347e/i3347e.pdf
6. Sophie Chao, 'Forest Peoples: Numbers across the world,' Forest Peoples Programme, 2012, http://www.forestpeoples.org/sites/fpp/files/publication/2012/05/forest-peoples-numbers-across-world-final_0.pdf
7. 'Overview,' WWF, Last accessed April 18 2020, https://www.worldwildlife.org/habitats/forest-habitat
8. Tariq Khokhar and Mahyar Eshragh Tabary, 'Five forest figures for the International Day of Forests,' World Bank Blogs, March 21 2016, https://blogs.worldbank.org/opendata/five-forest-figures-international-day-forests
9. 'About Us,' Canopy, Last accessed April 18 2020, https://canopyplanet.org/about-us/
10. 'Ancient Forest Friendly™,' Canopy, Last accessed April 18 2020, https://canopyplanet.org/solutions/ancient-forest-friendly/

11. Nathalie Remy, Eveline Speelman and Steven Swartz, 'Style that's sustainable: a new fast-fashion formula,' McKinsey, October 20 2016, https://www.mckinsey.com/business-functions/sustainability/our-insights/style-thats-sustainable-a-new-fast-fashion-formula

12. 'How much do our wardrobes cost the environment?' World Bank, September 23 2019, https://www.worldbank.org/en/news/feature/2019/09/23/costo-moda-medio-ambiente

13. Stephen Leahy, *Your Water Footprint* (Richmond Hill, Canada: Firefly Books, 2014)

CHAPTER 6

14. Robert Crotti et al, 'Global Gender Gap 2020,' *World Economic Forum*, 2020, p.6, http://www3.weforum.org/docs/WEF_GGGR_2020.pdf

15. 'Global Gender Gap Report, World Economic Forum, December 16 2019, http://www3.weforum.org/docs/WEF_GGGR_2020.pdf

16. 'Number of rough sleepers in England soars by 165% since 2010,' Crisis, January 31 2019, https://www.crisis.org.uk/about-us/media-centre/number-of-rough-sleepers-in-england-soars-by-165-since-2010/

17. 'Total Wealth in Great Britain: April 2016 to March 2018,' Office for National Statistics, December 5 2019, https://www.ons.gov.uk/peoplepopulationandcommunity/personalandhouseholdfinances/incomeandwealth/bulletins/totalwealthingreatbritain/april2016tomarch2018

18. Jo Cox MP, Maiden Speech at the Houses of Parliament (UK), June 3 2015

19. Cesar Busatto, as quoted by Roopinder Oberoi and Jamie P Halsall, *Revisiting Globalization: From a Borderless to a Gated Globe* (New York: Springer, 2018), p.121

20. 'Mexico 2012,' Homeless World Cup, Last accessed April 18 2020, https://homelessworldcup.org/mexico-2012/#:~:text=The%202012%20Homeless%20World%20Cup,ladies%20won%20the%20women's%20competition

21. 'Our Impact,' Homeless World Cup, Last accessed April 18 2020, https://homelessworldcup.org/our-impact/

22. *Ibid.*

CHAPTER 7

23. James Sloam and Muhammad Rakib Ehsan, 'Youth Quake: Young people and the 2017 General Election,' *Intergenerational Foundation, accessed via the British Library*, No. 11, November 26 2017, https://www.bl.uk/collection-items/youth-quake-young-people-and-the-2017-general-election

24. 'Facts & Figures,' UN Women, Last accessed March 20 2020, https://www.unwomen.org/en/news/in-focus/commission-on-the-status-of-women-2012/facts-and-figures

25. 'World's Women 2015,' UN Statistics Division, Department of Economic and Social Affairs, October 20 2015, https://unstats.un.org/unsd/gender/worldswomen.html

26. 'How Britain voted in 2015,' Ipsos MORI, August 26 2015, https://www.ipsos.com/ipsos-mori/en-uk/how-britain-voted-2015

27. James Sloam and Muhammad Rakib Ehsan, 'Youth Quake: Young people and the 2017 General Election,' *Intergenerational Foundation, accessed via the British Library*, No. 11, November 26 2017, https://www.bl.uk/collection-items/youth-quake-young-people-and-the-2017-general-election

CHAPTER 8

28. 'Income Inequality in the United States,' Inequality.org, Last accessed March 31 2020, https://inequality.org/facts/income-inequality/

29. Professor Anthony Shorrocks, Professor Jim Davies and Dr Rodrigo Lluberas, 'Global wealth report 2019,' *Credit Suisse,* No. 13, (October 2019), https://www.credit-suisse.com/about-us/en/reports-research/global-wealth-report.html

30. 'Global Inequality,' Inequality.org, accessed 31/03/2020, https://inequality.org/facts/global-inequality/

31. 'Inequality and Health,' Inequality.org, Last accessed March 31 2020, https://inequality.org/facts/inequality-and-health/

32. 'Gini Index,' The World Bank DataBank, Last accessed March 31 2020, https://databank.worldbank.org/reports.aspx?source=2&series=SI.POV.GINI&country=#

33. 'Inequality and Health,' Inequality.org, Last accessed March 31 2020, https://inequality.org/facts/inequality-and-health/

34. 'Unleashing the power of the poor,' Grameen Foundation, Last accessed April 1 2020, https://grameenfoundation.org/about-us/why-grameen

35. 'Breaking the vicious cycle of poverty through microcredit,' Grameen Bank, Last accessed April 31 2020, http://www.grameen.com/breaking-the-cycle-of-proverty/

36. Brice McKeever, 'The Nonprofit Sector in Brief,' National Center for Charitable Statistics (NCCS), January 3 2019, https://nccs.urban.org/project/nonprofit-sector-brief

CHAPTER 9

37. 'World conflict deaths,' Our World in Data, Last accessed April 5 2020, https://ourworldindata.org/grapher/world-conflict-deaths-various-sources?time=1402

38. Amanda Macias, 'From Aruba to Iceland, these 36 nations have no standing military,' *CNBC*, April 3 2018, https://www.cnbc.com/2018/04/03/countries-that-do-not-have-a-standing-army-according-to-cia-world-factbook.html

39. 'Covid-19 Dashboard,' Center for Systems Science and Engineering (CSSE) at John Hopkins University, Last accessed June 7 2020, https://coronavirus.jhu.edu/map.html

40. 'Syrian Revolution NINE years on: 586,100 persons killed and millions of Syrians displaced and injured,' The Syrian Observatory for Human Rights, 14 March 2020, https://www.syriahr.com/en/?p=157193&__cf_chl_jschl_tk__

41. 'Healthcare not Warfare infographic,' Global Campaign on Military Spending, April 15 2020, http://demilitarize.org/resources_categories/infographics_materials/

42. 'United States,' Worldometer, Last updated June 7 2020, https://www.worldometers.info/coronavirus/country/us/

43. Counter-Extremism Directorate, 'Counter-Extremism Strategy,' *HM Government*, No. 9 (October 2015), https://assets.publishing.service.gov.uk/government/uploads/system/uploads/attachment_data/file/470088/51859_Cm9148_Accessible.pdf

44. 'Number of fatalities due to terrorist attacks worldwide between 2006 and 2018,' Statista, October 2019, https://www.statista.com/statistics/202871/number-of-fatalities-by-terrorist-attacks-worldwide/

45. 'Facts and figures: Ending violence against women,' UN Women, Last accessed April 15 2020, https://www.unwomen.org/en/what-we-do/ending-violence-against-women/facts-and-figures

46. Mireille Widmer and Irene Pavesi et al, 'A Gendered Analysis of Violent Deaths,' *Small Arms Survey Research Notes*, No. 63, (November 2016), http://www.smallarmssurvey.org/fileadmin/docs/H-Research_Notes/SAS-Research-Note-63.pdf

CHAPTER 10

47. 'Two Decades of Impact: 2020 Impact Report,' *Schwab Foundation for Social Entrepreneurship, No. 21,* (January 2020), http://www3.weforum.org/docs/WEF_Schwab_Foundation_2020_Impact_Report.pdf

Author biographies

Mel Young MBE is a social entrepreneur and founder of several successful social enterprises including the Homeless World Cup, which uses football to inspire people who are homeless to transform their own lives; more than a million people have been positively impacted. He has won several awards and is the author of two books.

Alexandra Matthews' background is in writing and marketing; she also worked at Ashoka UK, a network of leading social innovators, where Mel is a Fellow. Together, they have created The New Ism, a discussion forum with a huge ambition: to create a new, more inclusive and sustainable global system that brings together the efforts of social innovators across the world.

Book summary

There's a lot going wrong in the world: climate change, war, inequality, divisive politics. It can be hard to see a way out of the issues we face. But social entrepreneurs across the world are addressing these big problems in innovative ways: The New Ism seeks to build their innovations into the fabric of modern society, creating a new, more sustainable and inclusive global system.

In this first book of a series on how society can learn from social innovators, authors Mel Young and Alexandra Matthews demystify what it means to be a social entrepreneur and explore how their work could help us all to create a sustainable, inclusive world where humans live within the means of the planet and all life can thrive. Through their podcast interviewing social innovators and disruptors, and Mel's experience as a leading social entrepreneur himself, they have a unique vantage point on what could be the key to a brighter future.